Shiro

KYOTO

GINZA

SEATTLE

SHIRO

**WIT, WISDOM
& RECIPES
FROM A
SUSHI PIONEER**

A MEMOIR BY
SHIRO KASHIBA

CHIN MUSIC PRESS
SEATTLE
WINTER 2011

Copyright © 2011
Recipes by Shiro Kashiba
Translation by Bruce Rutledge & Yuko Enomoto
Food Photos & Portraits by Ann Norton

CHIN MUSIC PRESS
2621 24th Ave W
Seattle, WA 98199-3407

www.chinmusicpress.com

Art Direction, Design & Illustration by Joshua Powell
Calligraphy by Ritsuko Kashiba
Text set in Mr. & Mrs. Eaves
Printed in China with Asia Pacific Offset

Photos on pages 136 (UW 26323z & UW 15716z) and 166 (UW 29694z) courtesy of
University of Washington Libraries, Special Collections. Photos on pages 168-169
(Images 77925 & 77926) courtesy of Seattle Municipal Archives.

ISBN 978-0984457625

Library of Congress Cataloging in Publication Data available.

PERILS OF PUBLISHING
On this job, we drank sake from a Dungeness crab shell. We learned how to clean
a smelt with our fingers. We touched a real live sea urchin. We watched Shiro pull
seaweed out of Shilshole Bay. We ate salmon skin that tasted like bacon. But we also
learned that this bounty will not last if we don't preserve it. We need to say goodbye
to bluefin, hello to albacore; eat local and/or sustainable; support the local fishermen;
savor this region's offerings and not worry about shipping in delicacies from afar. If
we don't, our bounty will disappear. Let's savor the fishies that didn't need a jet to get
here. And remember: fish poop helps slow global warming. —CMP

To the people of Washington state,
for allowing me to cook
for them for forty-five years.
Nothing makes me happier.

JAPAN

The Pacific Northwest

RECITES

SPRING

SUMMER

MULTI-SEASONAL

FALL

WINTER

春　夏

秋　冬

SHIRO'S TIPS, ETC.

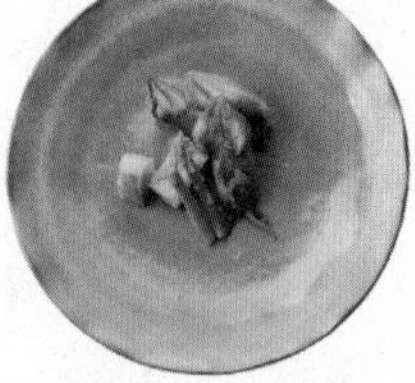

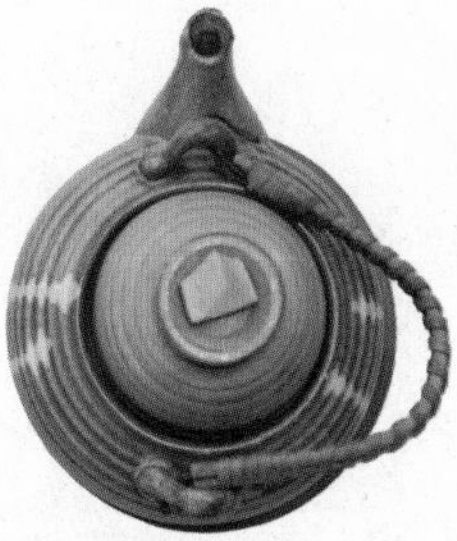

TRANSLATOR'S NOTE

FOR MUCH OF 2010, we would look forward to 11 AM on every other Tuesday, when we would meet Shiro Kashiba at his eponymous restaurant in Belltown and talk about sushi. He had contacted Misa Cartier, the publisher of *Ibuki* magazine, about producing a cookbook that would celebrate the bounty of the Pacific Northwest. As he approached his seventies, Shiro — not an overly reflective guy — was starting to look back on his life and his career. He wanted to share what he had learned, and he wanted to say thank you to his customers before it was too late (although he has no thoughts of retiring). Ms. Cartier put us in touch with Shiro, and we agreed to talk with him and see what developed.

The conversations were in Japanese, with English sprinkled in. Over time, the conversations became more personal, and we began to get to know the man behind the counter. We met his wife and son, his staff. He brought in boxes of family photographs and ephemera from his early days in Seattle: menus, matchbooks, brochures from swinging 70s go-go bars. We learned that he liked to climb trees, play golf, drink Bud Lite. We found that he had a license to pull seaweed out of the Puget Sound and that he had baked his own wedding cake. A photo he took during his early days in Seattle showed the then podunk skyline (The Smith Tower, the Space Needle and the oversized Seattle-First National Bank Building). It made us realize that the trajectory of his career paralleled the rise of Seattle.

Over the course of our conversations, we became convinced that this book should be more than a cookbook — it should be an intimate look at Shiro, his craft and the place

he chose to practice it for more than four decades. With the help of photographer Ann Norton, designer Josh Powell and Shiro's son, Ed Kashiba, we photographed Shiro in natural settings, behind the counter and in the kitchen, then sifted through boxes of family photos and pestered the Kashibas with questions about this sister or that childhood friend. To their great credit, the Kashibas never shut their door on us.

On the occasional photo shoot, Shiro would come alive as he walked the beaches of Ballard or the forests of Discovery Park. He would hop up on fallen trees, breathe in the fresh air and exclaim, "I love the outdoors." You couldn't help but think that this slight man from Kyoto, a man one Seattle magazine had described as "impish," was meant to spend his life in the Pacific Northwest.

But Shiro, by his own admission, has not become all that Americanized. When we asked him if he misses Japan, he answered, "Why should I? I work in a Japanese restaurant, have a Japanese wife, I speak Japanese all day, I eat Japanese food." His experience is not that of the Japanese Americans in town. Nor is it the typical experience of a Japanese expat. He is of a generation that saw great poverty in Japan and found ways to overcome that hardship. His way was to gamble that the people of Seattle would learn to love sushi. Boy, was he right.

Perhaps one reason Shiro is such a great chef is that he doesn't let himself get distracted from his core task. Each year, he is invited to serve sushi at Bill Gates' CEO Summit. After the 2010 summit, we asked him what it was like to meet Warren Buffett, the Princess of Monaco and all the other VIPs and corporate titans who were milling around Mr. Gates' mansion for the event. He stared blankly at us. Then he asked us if those people were really there. It never seemed to have dawned on him that he was serving the Masters and Mistresses of the Universe.

Or on a trip to a local market, Shiro hopped into the company pickup truck and pulled out of the parking lot, rap music blaring on the radio, the heavy bass line practically shaking the truck. After a few blocks, we finally had to ask him: "Do you like this music?" "Oh that?" he asked as if no-

ticing it for the first time. He promptly turned the radio off, and we drove on in silence.

But Shiro is not oblivious to his surroundings. He just chooses his points of focus. He's extremely proud to call local luminaries such as the Seattle Symphony's Gerard Schwarz, Ichiro Suzuki of the Mariners and glass maestro Lino Tagliapietra regulars of his restaurant. He is also eloquent when speaking about the culture of sushi and where it is headed in the US and back home in Japan. It is in these conversations — the conversations about the future of traditional sushi-making — that Shiro seems most wistful.

Shiro wants to offer a love letter to the Pacific Northwest. To go beyond the typical memoir/cookbook format, we asked Ritsuko Kashiba to share her calligraphy talents (see the four seasons on the table of contents and her other work in chapters two and nine), Josh Powell curated Shiro's personal photographs and ephemera, while also creating many illustrations and charts and Ann Norton spent a year skillfully documenting Shiro and his cooking in each of the four seasons. We hope you enjoy this intimate look at his life as much as we enjoyed making it.

Bruce Rutledge & Yuko Enomoto
SEATTLE
SUMMER 2011

CHAPTER ONE

SHUN

SHUN (shoo-n) n. the season.
海胆は今旬だ。 *Sea urchin is now in season.*

Shun. This word has been my guiding light as a sushi chef.
Put simply, it means "in season." But as I traveled from my
birthplace in Kyoto to the Ginza district of Tokyo, where I
started my career, and eventually to Seattle, the word began
to take on greater meaning. Once I settled in the Pacific
Northwest more than four decades ago, I began to see what
shun truly means. The bounty of this region is astonishing.
Rarities that demand top dollar in Asia were plentiful here:
the long, odd-looking geoduck lay ignored deep in the ocean
floor when I first arrived in Seattle; the spiny but succulent
sea urchin in the Pacific Northwest is the most delicious
I have ever tasted; ocean smelt, such a versatile fish and
relatively unknown in Japan, is everywhere; tasty ferns that
Japanese covet grow wild in the roughs of my favorite golf
courses. The riches of this region quickly turned me into a
locavore. It also gave me the edge I needed to survive in the
brutal restaurant business. For more than forty years, I sur-
vived by using local ingredients to build my reputation and
recover my losses. I found that the local bounty was more
delicious and more affordable than anything I could fly in
from Japan; thus I began to change the way I served sushi —
and I believe that change brought me closer to the roots
of sushi.

When I came to Seattle in 1966, there wasn't a sushi bar
anywhere. Locals ate some rolls, for sure, but a fully operat-
ing sushi bar as we know it today didn't exist yet.

Shun.
Calligraphy by Ritsuko
Kashiba.

OPPOSITE
Shiro pulls kelp out of
Shilshole Bay.

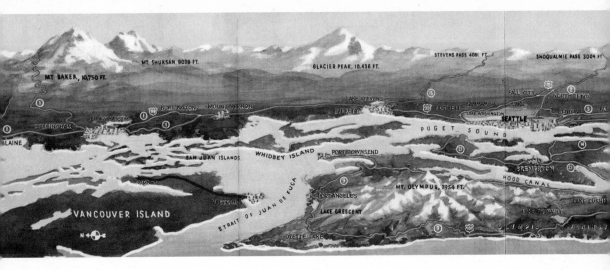

Fast forward to 2011 and sushi is as American as apple pie (a dish that's near to my heart, but that's a story for a later chapter). While I am thrilled that Japanese cuisine has been embraced by North Americans, I'm also a bit worried about where it's all headed. I'm worried that the bounty of the Pacific Northwest is not completely appreciated by its residents, which makes it easier for others to exploit. The geoduck burrowed into the sands of the Puget Sound, for example, is becoming harder and harder to find as more of it is being sucked out with vacuum tubes and exported to East Asia for increasingly exorbitant prices. I don't want the Puget Sound's bounty to be exhausted. We need to conserve and respect our resources if we want them to last.

Sushi fans may have heard the term Edomae sushi. This is the classical fare most people think of when they hear the word "sushi." A slab of bluefin, some yellowtail, a thin slice of octopus, sweet egg wrapped in seaweed, a shrimp, a piece of eel slathered in sauce and a pile of sliced ginger on the side. This meal has been replicated all over the world. But as I started to understand the bounty of the Puget Sound region, I began reflecting on that phrase: Edomae sushi. Edo was the original name of Tokyo. The term *mae* means "front." Edomae originally meant food pulled out of Edo Bay, today's Tokyo Bay. As Edomae sushi flourished and began to be served throughout Japan, and later, the world, the

original meaning became less and less important. And today, sushi pulled from the polluted and heavily trafficked Tokyo Bay may sound like a sick joke. But back then, Edo Bay was teeming with fish. It had a bounty not unlike the one of my adopted home in the Pacific Northwest.

Over the years, the idea of replicating Edomae sushi for my North American customers seemed an increasingly arcane exercise. Why fly in the delicious but over-fished bluefin when equally delicious albacore could be bought from the fishing boats and specialty markets here? Why not add more indigenous oysters to the menu? And let's not forget my beloved ocean smelt. I became so enamored of the versatile, inexpensive and tasty fish that I once prepared a ten-course ocean-smelt dinner for my guests.

As the years went on, I replaced Edomae with Puget Sound-mae, or more accurately, Pacific Northwest-mae. Sourcing local ingredients gave me the edge I needed to survive in a cutthroat business. And, if I do say so myself, the local fare tastes better.

But let me be clear: I am about as traditional of a sushi chef as there is. In sushi, the simple taste is best. This is the most important point in understanding Japanese cuisine. Simple, fresh, local. These are my touchstones. And this is what *shun* means to me.

A few years ago, two hearty fellows in cowboy hats came

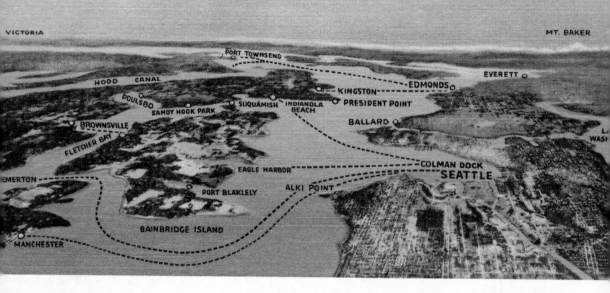

VICTORIA — MT. BAKER

PORT TOWNSEND

EVERETT

HOOD CANAL — EDMONDS

POULSBO — KINGSTON — PRESIDENT POINT

SANDY HOOK PARK — SUQUÁMISH — INDIANOLA BEACH

BROWNSVILLE — BALLARD

FLETCHER BAY

EAGLE HARBOR — COLMAN DOCK — SEATTLE

EMERTON — PORT BLAKLELY — ALKI POINT

BAINBRIDGE ISLAND

MANCHESTER

LA WASH

See *All* of the

BEAUTIFUL
PACIFIC
NORTHWEST

into my restaurant and ordered a couple of fusion rolls. I politely explained that Shiro's isn't the best place for that kind of sushi and pointed them in the direction of a restaurant I thought they would like. I'm not sure what they thought of having their business turned down, but I hope they found what they were looking for. At Shiro's, it's about preserving tradition, but it's also about infusing that tradition with fresh life. Seattle is a wonderful place for me to do just that.

In these pages, I aim to demystify Japanese cuisine by offering easy-to-follow recipes. I also celebrate the bounty of the Pacific Northwest and tell how I came to fall in love with this region. But more than anything else, I want to express my gratitude to the people of the Pacific Northwest and the out-of-towners who come by my restaurant when they're in Seattle. I have been humbled beyond words at the way my life has turned out. I know it sounds corny, but I'm an immigrant who still speaks English with an accent and you've allowed me to live the American Dream. Thank you.

1965

KYOTO, JAPAN

2010

SEATTLE, USA

→

1941

BORN IN KYOTO, JAPAN

1945

WWII ENDS

1959

GRADUATES HIGH SCHOOL

1960

MOVES TO TOKYO,
WORKS AT YOSHINO
RESTAURANT

SANJA FESTIVAL

TOKYO

YOSHINO RESTAURANT

BASEBALL TEAM

MT. MIHARA
IZU OSHIMA ISLAND

KIYOSATO
YAMANASHI PREFECTURE

YATSUGATAKE MOUNTAINS
BORDER OF NAGANO & YAMANASHI
PREFECTURES

MT. TANIGAWA

GUNMA PREFECTURE

1966

MOVES TO US TO WORK
AT TANAKA RESTAURANT

1970

OPENS FIRST FULL SERVICE
SUSHI BAR IN SEATTLE
AT MANEKI RESTAURANT

FIRST CAR
1969 TOYOTA CORONA

WEDDING CEREMONY
JAPAN

1970

MARRIES RITSUKO

WEDDING CEREMONY
SEATTLE BUDDHIST CHURCH

1971

SON EDWIN BORN

1972

OPENS OWN RESTAURANT

SALMON FISHING
SITKA, ALASKA

1986
OPENS HANA, FIRST
CONVEYOR-BELT SUSHI RESTAURANT
IN SEATTLE

1991
SELLS NIKKO TO
WESTIN HOTEL, BECOMES
EXECUTIVE CHEF AT
NEW RESTAURANT

PULLING KELP
SHILSHOLE BAY, SEATTLE

1993
RETIRES, SPENDS
YEAR TRAVELING

1994
OPENS SHIRO'S

2011

SHIRO'S RENOVATED

JOURNEY

CHAPTER TWO

GIVE ME CHOCOLATE

I WAS BORN on July 22, 1941, in the city of Kyoto. I was four when World War II ended. Our hometown, the cultural heart of Japan, was spared the bombing that so much of the country had endured, so I had little understanding of what an historic time it was for my country. When the American GIs rolled into town, I thought they were just about the coolest guys I had ever seen. My friends and I would run after them yelling, "*Gibu me chocoreto*." They seemed to have an endless supply of chocolate and candy to dole out to us hungry kids.

Compared to the rest of Japan, we had it relatively easy during those early postwar days. My father was an elementary school principal and my mother was a homemaker. I guess you could say we were a middle-class family. I had two sisters and a brother growing up. I was in the middle, with an older sister and brother and a younger sister to play with.

However, there was quite an age gap between my older siblings and I. My sister was nine years older than me, and my brother was six years older. That meant that my playmate was usually my younger sister, Mitsuko. We used to play in the hills around our house, hike through the woods and go mushroom picking. We used to go swimming with our schoolmates too.

I still go back to Kyoto at least once a year and have lots of strong ties there despite living most of my life in Seattle. In fact, we still hold reunions for our elementary school. I'm usually the one traveling the farthest to return for the party, but more often than not, I still get stuck cooking for everybody.

OPPOSITE

My childhood home in Kyoto, which still stands today. It replaced the original Kashiba home, a traditional wooden structure. With the constant fear of fire bombings during the war, many wooden homes were ordered to be demolished.

OPPOSITE

The view from my childhood home in Kyoto.

LEFT

My grandmother holds me for the family portrait with my parents, brother and sister.

ABOVE

With my younger sister and playmate Mitsuko.

BELOW

My father waits for the train.

When I was growing up, my dad used to say that some day one of us children would go to America. I don't know why he said that or what was behind the thought, but his words stuck in my mind. Those cool GIs with the free chocolate were from America. What else was over there?

Every once in a while, my mom and dad would take us to the local sushi shop. Back then, sushi was an expensive meal, and especially in the days after World War II, it was often out of the price range of most families. While the Kashiba family wasn't rich, my dad had a steady job and we could afford to visit the local sushi shop every once in awhile.

While dad ate a plate of sashimi, the children would eat *tamago* (sweet egg) or other cheaper items on the menu. Sushi looked different then in some respects. The endangered bluefin, whose fatty toro slabs are the ultimate to many sushi lovers today, wasn't even eaten back then. The Japanese thought it was too fatty and unappetizing.

I loved going to the local sushi shop. The food was fine — as a child, I didn't appreciate sushi like I would later in life. The real highlight for me was the chef behind the counter. He wore white, had a headrag over his hair and wielded his knives so expertly and precisely, it practically hypnotized me. He looked so cool, confident and in control. And what he did seemed to please his customers to no end. I wish I could

OPPOSITE
At the top of Daimonjiyama in Kyoto.

LEFT
Mom, Dad, Mitsuko and I visiting the family cemetery in my father's hometown of Ayabe, in the mountains of northern Kyoto.

BELOW
The entire family.

FOLLOWING PAGES
My high school, located behind the famous Nijo Castle.

remember his name, but the image of that chef stayed in my mind as I grew up.

As I got older, I continued to appreciate the energy and vigor of the sushi shop. I realized early on that a sushi chef was also a performer. The way he stood, his attitude toward the customer and the way he made each piece of sushi exuded a quiet confidence that put the customers at ease. He always had his containers of rice, *wasabi* and *gari*, or pickled ginger, placed to his right as he faced the cutting board. His knives lay in front of him, just past the board. He had a wet cloth he used to wipe the board from time to time, and he would wring out the cloth after each series of wipes. He had a bowl of *tezu* (slightly vinegary water) to dip his hands into and keep the rice from sticking. He worked deftly but never seemed to be distracted from his customers. He'd quickly compile pieces of sushi, arrange them on a tray ever so precisely and add a garnish of some sort called a *tsuma* to make sure the customers have a feast for their eyes before they even taste the sushi. Then he would place the tray in front of my father or the other customers at the bar.

The process was so involved and precise, it enthralled me. Plus, I've always been a gregarious fellow, and the friendly confidence of the chefs appealed to me. I didn't have a clue at the time how hard the work would turn out to be and how much preparation is necessary to be a good sushi chef, but

OPPOSITE
Hiking around the hills and
forests of Kyoto.

TOP LEFT
With Mitsuko and a family
friend at a shrine in my father's
hometown.

BELOW
Getting ready to practice the
clarinet.

the way our local chef carried himself as he served his customers was enough to whet my appetite.

As I entered my teens, I started to think about apprenticing at a sushi shop, which was the way you started in those days. But my parents insisted that I finish high school first. I dutifully did as I was told, but the conviction kept growing inside of me that my career would be in sushi. And while I will always love Kyoto, I really wanted to go to Tokyo to study in the home of Edomae sushi, the most popular style of sushi in Japan.

Once I graduated high school, I began to figure out how to live my dream. A family acquaintance who worked in Tokyo promoting Kyoto's Kiyomizu-yaki pottery introduced me to a sushi bar looking for an apprentice. It was a venerable, traditional sushi restaurant on the Ginza. The perfect spot to start my career. Pretty soon, I was packing my bags for Tokyo.

Looking back, it's strange to think that my life's path was being set at such a young age. The two coolest types of people in my mind were the GIs with their chocolate and the sushi chefs with their sharp knives and their quiet confidence. Two decades later, I would find myself behind the counter of a sushi bar in the US, serving Americans, perhaps even former GIs who developed a taste for fish while occupying my country. Imagine! At the age of four or so, the seeds for my future were firmly planted.

KYOTO

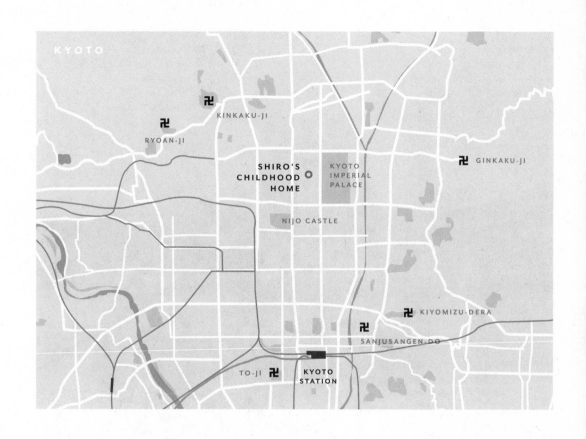

KYOTO

KINKAKU-JI

RYOAN-JI

SHIRO'S
CHILDHOOD
HOME

KYOTO
IMPERIAL
PALACE

GINKAKU-JI

NIJO CASTLE

KIYOMIZU-DERA

SANJUSANGEN-DO

TO-JI

KYOTO
STATION

Swimming in the Kizu River during
my elementary school days.

05
I took this photo of fishermen
on Lake Suwa while traveling
in Nagano Prefecture.

06
Playing reveille while facing
toward Kyoto.

03

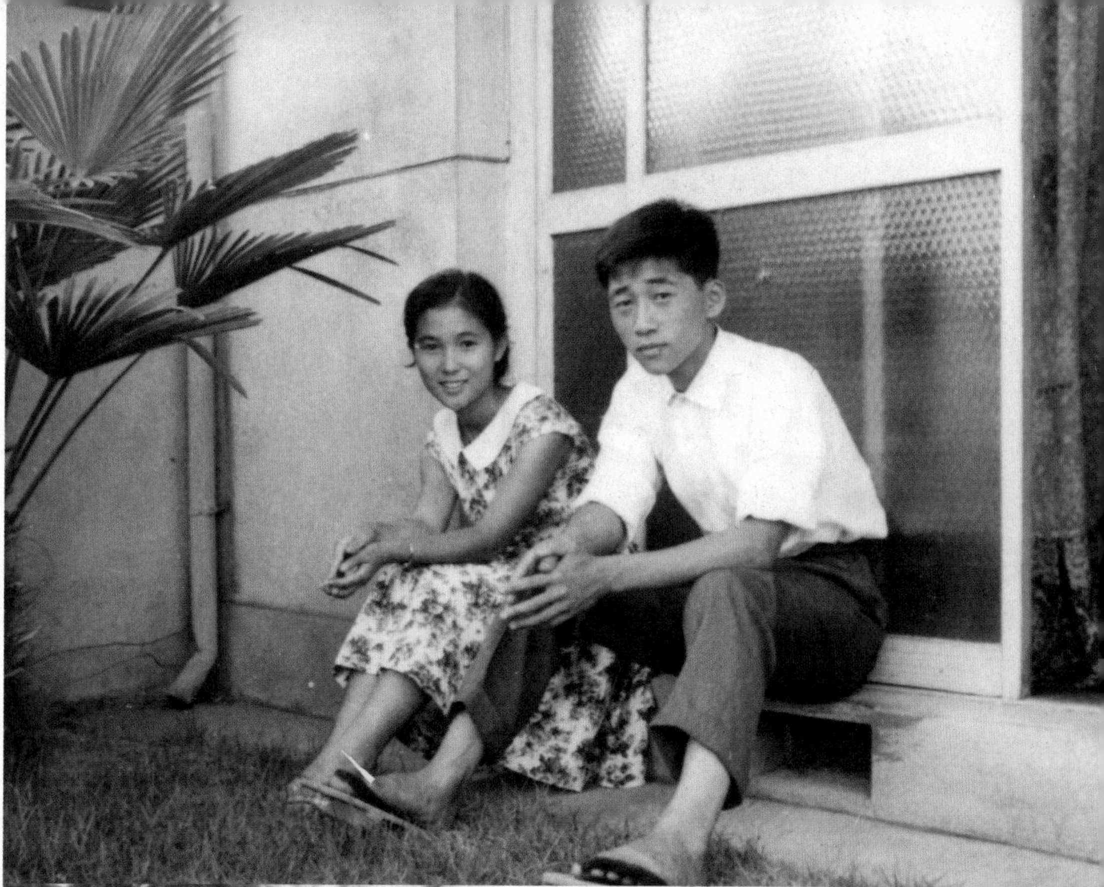

04

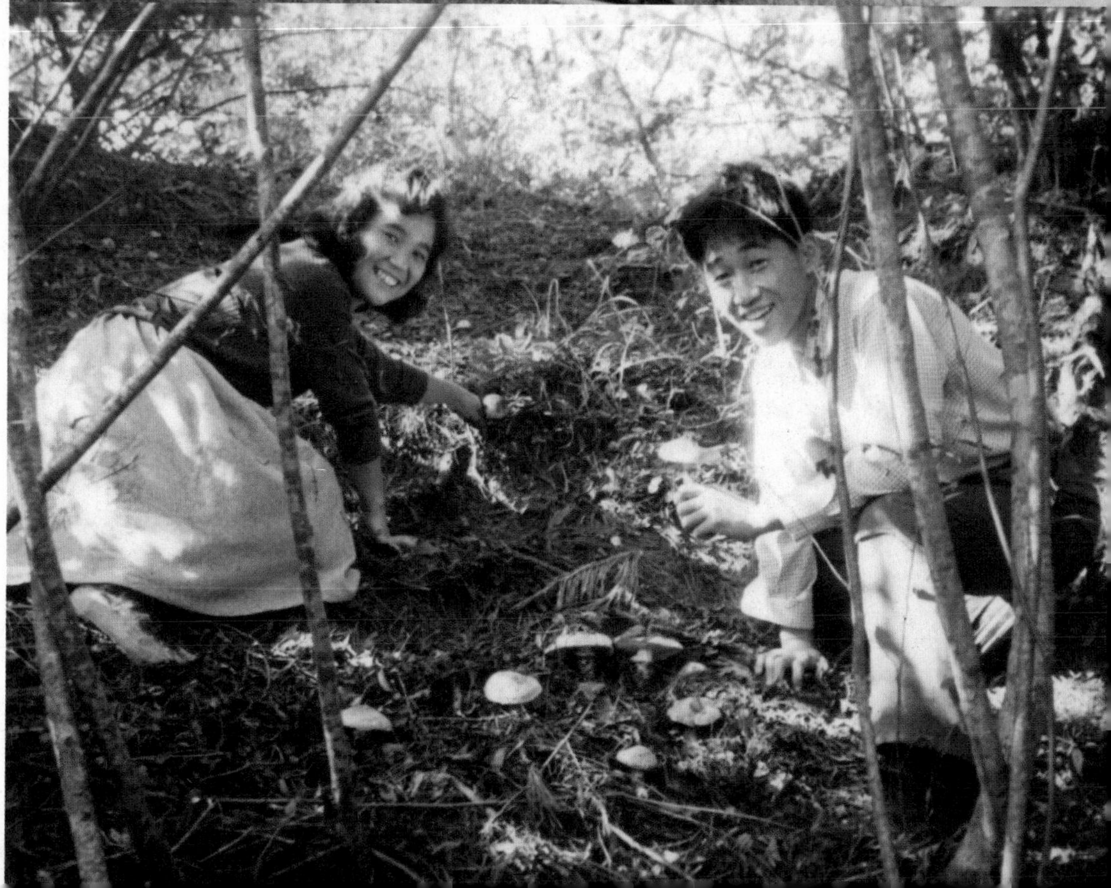

CHAPTER THREE

AN EYE FOR FISH

MY FIRST JOB was at Yoshino Hontenzushi, which is still in operation today near the Kyobashi intersection in Tokyo's Ginza district, perhaps the poshest neighborhood in all of Japan in those days. It was a thrill to work there because it was one of the original restaurants to serve Edomae sushi. I knew I would learn a lot, but I also knew the apprenticeship wouldn't be easy.

The apprentice system in Japan has fallen out of favor for the most part, but in the 1950s and 1960s, it was still the way you learned your trade, whether you wanted to be a chef, swordsmith, carpenter or even a baseball player. You put in your hard work on menial tasks at first and were expected to pick up little clues from the masters in your midst. The masters wouldn't really teach us so much as just go about their regular business and expect us to watch them like hawks, picking up whatever tips and insights we could. Little by little, the apprentice would learn the trade, often spending years, even decades, doing the tasks Americans might term "thankless." But since everyone started this way, there was no room to whine. The master chefs behind the sushi bar also had put in their time sweeping up, cooking rice in the back and cleaning fish.

When I arrived in Tokyo, I knew that I would work hard, receive little pay and be expected to learn from the masters. It never dawned on me that I should get more pay or receive more days off (I worked six days a week) — I felt honored to get to see sushi masters such as Jiro Ono ply their craft.

In fact, as of this writing, Jiro Ono is still serving sushi in the Ginza at age eighty-five. His restaurant received three

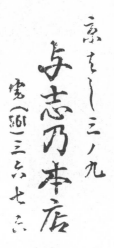

ABOVE
Letterhead from the stationery used at Yoshino Hontenzushi.

OPPOSITE TOP
With the other staff in front of the entrance to Yoshino.

**OPPOSITE BOTTOM &
FOLLOWING PAGES**
Performing chores during my apprenticeship.

Michelin stars and he has even been honored by the emperor as a living national treasure. I consider him a friend and mentor. If you draw a line from me to him, and then again from me to all of my former employees who have launched their own restaurants in the greater Seattle area (and there are many), then I guess you could say that sushi culture in Seattle has firm, traditional roots.

For the six and a half years I worked at Yoshino, I lived in the back of the restaurant or a separate dorm with the other apprentices. I didn't receive a formal salary, but I would always get some spending money for my day off. I ate my meals with the other staff and worked long hours. My life was as regimented as any military person's, but I was doing what I had always wanted: learning the sushi trade.

As part of our training, we would be forced to sit for hours in *seiza* style on hardwood floors. "*Seiza*" is written with the characters for "proper" and "sitting." You tuck your legs under your thighs and sit on your heels. We had to master this and be able to serve guests in tatami-mat rooms this way. If we showed any discomfort or complained about an ache in our legs, we failed, and failure was not an option. So we sat and sat and sat in *seiza* until it became second nature.

People familiar with Japanese culture will understand

OPPOSITE
Hiking on my day off. That's me on the left and Jiro Ono on the right.

ABOVE
Tokyo's Ginza district lit up in neon.

Yoshino-sensei — the big boss and my first employer.

how important sitting this way is — anyone practicing a martial art or Zen meditation or tea ceremony has to be able to sit this way too.

Other chores I had were to deliver sushi by bicycle through the streets of Tokyo. Often I'd be balancing several dishes piled high while manuevering through Tokyo traffic. It sounds like a big deal, but I was pretty good at it. I never had a problem darting through traffic while balancing plates of very expensive sushi. I'm glad I didn't think too much about my cargo back then or I might have gotten nervous.

I did have a problem with one thing, though: One day I was told to make the *dashi*, a vital part of Japanese cuisine. *Dashi* is a soup stock that provides the base for many Japanese dishes. It is often said to bring out the *umami*, or savoriness, in a dish. Ingredients typically include *katsuobushi* (dried bonito flake) or dried shiitake mushrooms or *konbu* (brown algae or seaweed). Of course, I know all this now, but at the time, I really didn't have a clue what *dashi* was.

I dutifully followed directions, heating water in a pan, putting the dried bonito flakes in the water just before it came to a boil, and then turning off the flame after ten seconds or so as the flakes sank down to the bottom of the pan. Then I dumped all the soup into the sink and walked over to the chefs with a clump of watered down *katsuobushi* in my strainer. "I have made the *dashi*," I announced.

Luckily, I kept my job. I guess I wasn't the first apprentice not to have a clue what I was doing. And I quickly learned that *dashi* is the soup, not the watered down ingredients used to make that soup. I still laugh when I think of what a *baka* (fool) I was that day.

Another chore I had during my apprenticeship was to go to the Tsukiji Fish Market a few times a week with the head chefs to pick out the fish for that day. This was one of the most educational aspects of my apprenticeship. Tsukiji Fish Market is a sprawling place filled with every kind of seafood you can imagine. It's the biggest fish market in the world. The market kicks off around four in the morning with the tuna auctions. This is a wild spectacle: men make mysterious hand gestures to bid on the fish as the fast-talking auctioneer keeps the bidding going at a frantic pace. If you ever go to

東 京 観 光 記 念　1965. 5. 23　はと⬤バス

Tokyo and suffer from jet lag and wake up at, say three-thirty in the morning, throw some clothes on and hop in a cab to Tsukiji to see it for yourself. You won't be disappointed.

Next to the auctions is a huge market with row after row of vendors peddling their seafood. Surrounding the market are old shops and restaurants that often fill up in the morning with workers and tourists. It's an energetic place. For six and a half years, I would come here with the masters at the crack of dawn and watch as they picked their fish for the day. I learned that when picking a larger fish, the body and the fins should have a shine to them. The eyes should be clear, not cloudy, and when you touch a gill and find a little blood there, that's a good sign. I still use these methods today when I do my shopping in Seattle. And I think it's fair to say that I've gotten a reputation for being one of the pickiest customers. My masters would be proud.

During my six and a half years working at Yoshino, I learned the skills I needed for success in the US. Today, I

The Yoshino staff (back row) took a night tour of Tokyo and were joined by some lovely ladies.

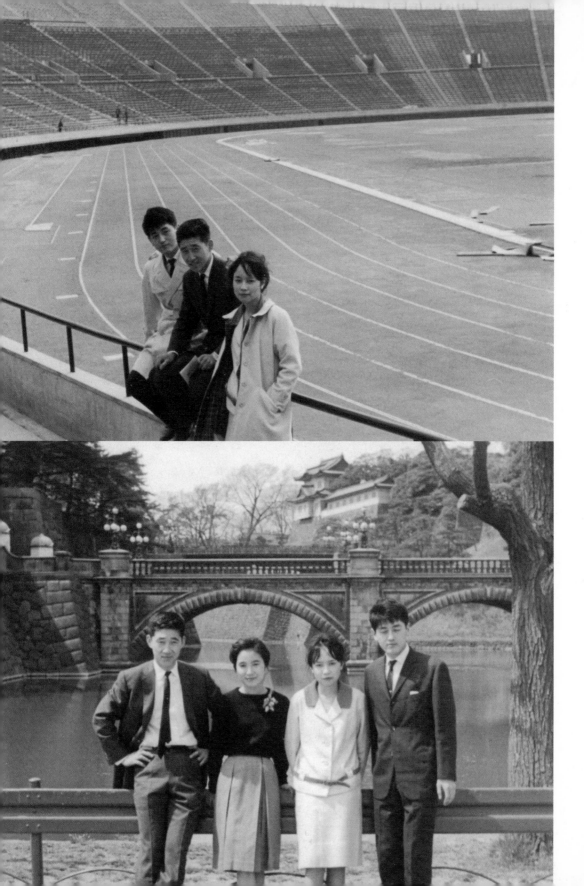

try to incorporate some of the old Japanese apprenticeship system into my Seattle restaurant — while complying with all current US labor laws, of course! I take my staff shopping so that they can learn how I pick out the fish. I make a point of eating lunch with the staff, too, and — since we're cooking the lunch in the restaurant before we open for dinner — talking with them about what tasted good and what needs improvement. Our lunch together is also a lesson for the staff in frugality. We use the parts of the fish left over after preparing dishes for the guests (what did you expect — I feed everyone sushi?), so we're scraping the last bits of flesh from the bone and using cuts that would otherwise get tossed away. Even when eating these parts of the fish, we can get a sense of the fish's overall quality and taste. Plus, the restaurant business is brutal — if my employees want to run their own businesses one day, they'll need to learn early that being frugal and resourceful with your material is key. This is something I learned at Yoshino.

But I have adapted my teaching methods to my staff, too. I do one thing that we didn't do in Japan: At the close of business, I tell the staff how we did financially that evening. I know that these young workers in my restaurant have aspirations like I had back in the 1960s. They probably want to open their own restaurant some day. And I want to give them all the tools they need to succeed.

OPPOSITE
Visiting the National Olympic Stadium and Tokyo Imperial Palace grounds with Mitsuko and friends.

ABOVE
Drinking and hiking with members of my hiking club.

TOKYO

TOKYO

SHINJUKU

SHIBUYA

GINZA

OTEMACHI
STATION

MITSUKOSHIMAE
STATION

NIHONBASHI
STATION

TOKYO
STATION

KYOBASHI
STATION

YOSHINO
HONTENZUSHI

YURAKUCHO
STATION

GINZA

Restaurant matchboxes from Yoshino (left) and
Sukiyabashi Jiro (right), which is run by Jiro Ono.
Back in the 1960s, it was Sukiyabashi Yoshino,
but Ono-san was allowed to take it over. He still
runs it today.

すきやばし浜し郎

五三五、三六〇〇

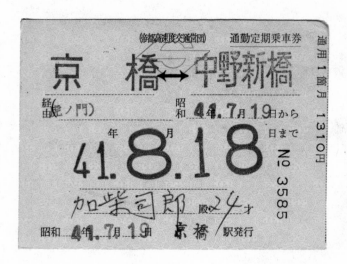

A train ticket showing my daily
commute between Kyobashi, where
Yoshino was located, and Nakano-
Shinbashi, where I lived with the
other staff.

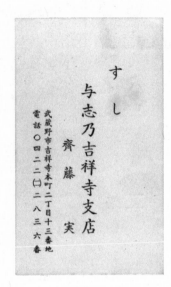
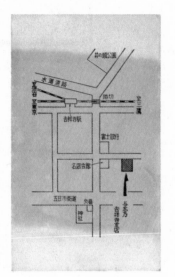

A business card and map of the
Yoshino Kichijoji branch, where I
often helped out.

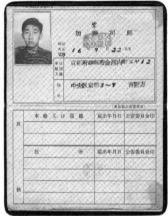

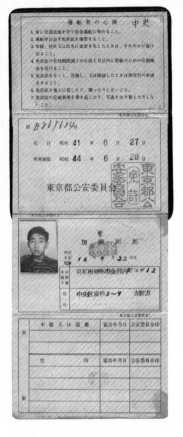

As a deliveryman for Yoshino, I
needed a driver's license for my
scooter. Licenses were a bit fancier
back in the 1960s.

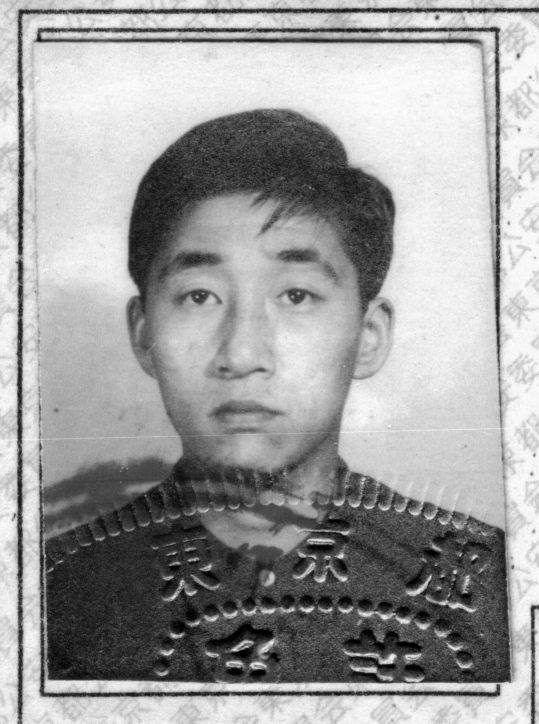

本籍又

明
大
昭

CHAPTER FOUR

SUSHI ON THE GINZA

SEVERAL YEARS INTO my apprenticeship, I was moved
out to the front counter to help prepare sushi in front of the
guests. I wasn't a full-fledged sushi chef yet, but this was a
big step for me. Suddenly, I could see the diners, hear their
conversations and watch their reactions to our cuisine.

A lot of the early customers were traders and business-
men. Many conducted international business. I began hear-
ing tales of "America," that place my dad had spoken of, and
the tales sounded pretty good. There was money to be made,
wide open spaces, a booming economy — or at least this is
what I heard. I was intrigued. Though I was still young and
inexperienced, my trip from Kyoto to Tokyo taught me that
I liked being on the move, adapting to new environments,
facing new challenges. Maybe I'd make my dad's predictions
come true.

But how to do that? I didn't have any contacts in the US,
and I knew very little about the country. There wasn't an
Internet to do research on or a directory of Japanese restaurants overseas to contact.

Luckily, I had a childhood friend who was getting ready
to backpack across the US during that time. Before he set out
on his trip, he asked me what sort of *omiyage* I wanted when
he returned. I had to give that some thought. What sort of
gift would I want from America?

The Japanese are always bearing gifts when they return
from a trip, and these gifts are referred to as *omiyage*. Typical
omiyage is a regional delicacy or a bottle of top-shelf Scotch
or a box of expensive chocolates. In Seattle during Japan's
bubble economy of the late 1980s and early 1990s, well-

heeled Japanese travelers would bring back beautifully packaged smoked salmon. We call these regional treats *meibutsu*, and Japan is filled with them (as is Seattle). Stop off at any major train station (and most minor ones) in Japan, and you'll find *meibutsu* (oranges and green tea from Shizuoka, soy sauce from Hokkaido, local sake along the western coast) all wrapped and ready to be purchased. But I digress.

Before my buddy headed out on his trip to the US, I made an odd request: For my *omiyage*, please bring back any information you can find about Japanese restaurants in America.

He came through. After spending months in the US, he returned with a long list of Japanese restaurants from all across the country and a bunch of chopstick wrappers and matchbooks with more addresses printed on them. This box of scraps was my link to the US.

I started writing letters to the addresses on these chopstick sleeves and matchbooks, asking if anyone out there needed an accomplished sushi chef. I admit I was full of youthful idealism, thinking this plan would bear fruit. I felt that American restaurateurs would at least give me credit for training at one of Japan's most respected sushi bars. After all, I was learning the trade in the home of sushi and in the heart of Japan's glitziest neighborhood, the Ginza. Someone out there would want to hire me, I thought.

I penned dozens of letters. After waiting for weeks and weeks, I finally got one solid response. It came from the pro-

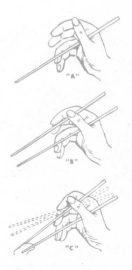

prietor of a Japanese restaurant in San Francisco. It was curt and to the point: "You need more experience."

I was humbled but not defeated. The idea of someday moving to the US and setting up a sushi bar had taken hold of me. The US was the land of our desires in the 1960s — it was free, wild and exciting, or at least that's how it seemed to a twentysomething man working six days a week, with no fixed salary and living in the back of a sushi restaurant. I was determined to figure out a way to live and work in the US.

At Yoshino, traders would share tales of doing business in the US. One regular customer traveled frequently to Seattle. He told me about his favorite place to eat there: Tanaka Restaurant, which was in the International District. I told him of my dream to live and work in the US. The customer told me that the next time he was in Seattle, he'd drop by Tanaka Restaurant and mention me. I thanked him, but didn't really expect anything to come of it. However, he kept his word, and a few months after our conversation, I was writing a letter to Mr. Tanaka to inquire about a position.

My younger readers should try to picture how relatively disconnected we were back then, well before the dawn of the Internet, and how slow things proceeded by today's standards. Mr. Tanaka and I exchanged letters for a couple of years before he eventually flew to Tokyo to meet me and offer me a job. The letters would take a week or two to be delivered, so if I heard back from Mr. Tanaka once a month, it was like getting an instant message!

One letter stands out for me. On August 27, 1965, he wrote to explain just how hard life in the US would be, and he warned me not to believe in this idea of an "American Dream." Here's an excerpt:

Thank you for your letter. I'm sorry my response has been late. I understand your passion well. After looking into the matter thoroughly, I believe the best way for you to come here is as a student. The conditions are as follows: five hours of studying at school every day (excluding Saturday and Sunday). You must attend classes in English. Then after classes are done, you would be able to study a subject of your

choice. There are classes offered here for cooks. The
issue is, are you up for the physical challenge of
studying from 8am to 2pm, then working until 11pm? The
next question is, are you willing to try everything?
Not just a sushi specialist? We are closed on Sundays,
so you will have the day off. You can golf or ski — do
whatever you want. The other thing is, how long you
plan on staying here. And, since you are planning on
working here, I want to make sure that you have a goal,
that you acquire something in terms of work before your
return. That's also the reason for your studies here,
but I emphasize that if you are to come all the way out
here, it has to be fruitful.

   Many people believe the United States is a country
of dreams, but you must never think of it that way. I
will begin the process for your trip here as soon as
you feel that you are really ready to struggle, feel
lonely and to bear through hardship after hardship.
I came here a decade ago with nothing more than the
clothes on my back. It was hardship after hardship. I
have worked eighteen-hour days. I am repeating myself,
but if you really feel confident about persisting
through a life of hardship, then write back. To put
it in an old-fashioned way, be ready to serve as a
manservant.

   Sincerely,
   Ted Tanaka

A "manservant." That's not exactly what I had envisioned
with life in the US, but I appreciated Tanaka-san's honesty.
I wrote back right away that I was up for the challenge, ready
to experience whatever America could throw at me.

   After I gained his trust through my consistent replies to
his questions, he agreed to hire me. Near the end of 1966,
the deal was done and I had a job waiting for me in Seattle.
Tanaka-san wrote to tell me to book a flight on Northwest
Orient Airlines. He'd be waiting at the airport for me.
Finally, at the age of twenty-five, I was headed to America.

OPPOSITE
Saying goodbye at Haneda
Airport.

FOLLOWING PAGES
One of the letters I received
from Ted Tanaka.

Ted T. Tanaka
1303-13th Ave. So.
Seattle, Wash. 98144, U.S.A.

Mr. Shiro Kashiba
Shinmachinishiiru
Shimochojamachi
Kamikyo-Ku, KYOTO-SHI
JAPAN

AÉROGRAMME ● PAR AVION

Ted T. Tanaka
1303-13th Ave. So.
Seattle, Wash. 98144, U.S.A.

Mr. Shiro Kashiba
Shinmachinishiiru
Shimochojamachi
Kamikyo-Ku, KYOTO-SHI
JAPAN

AÉROGRAMME ● PAR AVION

Ted T. Tanaka
1303-13th Ave. So.
Seattle, Wash. 98144, U.S.A.

SEATTLE
WASH.
NOV 09
PM
1966

Mr. Shiro Kashiba
Shinmachinishiiru
Shimochojamachi
Kamikyo-Ku, KYOTO-SHI
JAPAN

AÉROGRAMME • PAR AVION

京都市上立
下ちよう町
新町西入ル
加柴同前殿

当申
貴殿の友人に一度二井飯らの一お出の若もし
で是年を経過する人が有り毎一たら遇くべ心
いて下さい当左右之父と車と思よ一すべて
良い人が疲れるると来へてありすそう。お車を少し
重食も用意一たいと思にあらーお
現在は夕食より朝食に一つたすれば人気大変皆で庭座
するう方れば又年でらりかので無度らな程度に毎べて
見て下さい

後明連絡一すよ。
手た仕・ものが有るかー知れますが出来う大年く
知らせくくてもりつて。べはくらぐ一時両観
に良ろしく大度へ下さい。

武運走う事より得一へ祈と。

加柴君
岡中

拝啓

京都よりのお便り有難う。その後も元気で居らるる事と思いますが、当方も皆々元気にやって居ります。坂井殿へ渡米の期日で
すが先にも書きましたが、出来る丈早く渡米されるは一月の始めですが、学校に入学するには一月の始めですが

してfrom土地に剖れる車が（奈良いの）では無いかと思いますリー当る可き貴殿が
来てから度々方も改進したく思って居り、大分色々と色々約人用意をーーても
ろ利のですが凡を今も車に子一たら様に余り必要はないと思います。又大阪にも備へると
の車さえ心要す方と思って居り、貴殿には芝野にて経験も有るので当地に
ても色々と研究出来幸行すると思って子ーー
当飛行機の都件は十二日付で当地より

ノースウエスト航空にて電報にて
送りました。大阪支店へ行けば私の良く知って
いる人で須崎信子と云ふ人が居ります。
解る方車は間いて下さい。ミヤトルへ用年に行く
と申して居リーて下さい。ノースウエストからは先貴殿
に通知が有ると更にーー出来る丈早く渡米
する都に飛行機の都合を取って下さい。

切府行東京羽田より当地にーー下さい
お発国時えば日より当地までーー
近いに行けますーーノースウエストは毎日ー当地
直達家にて約八時間ですー何し人眠りは有ません
何度も幸まーーすが衣料品その他新潟等せめ
御心配け十て下さい次に小さの衍は小物（一生で二三
事いて大事ですが極牛（白梅牛）をーー食べたいの
で頼みまた、又出来ければ来て下さい
東京出発前にーーー宜って来て下さいそれに
事よの出発前に事よの友人の庭に立寄って持って
まてほしいすが有るからも先れません先て都合で米

Staying at a traditional inn during
an annual trip with the Yoshino
restaurant staff.

With some members of my hiking
and mountain-climbing club.

Photos from a trip to volcanic Oshima Island, part of the Izu island chain that extends south from Tokyo.

I was always struck by the beauty of
alpine flowers.

PRECEDING PAGES
More mountain-climbing adventures,
including a winter summit of Mt.
Yatsugatake.

DISCOVERY

CHAPTER FIVE

APPLE PIE À LA MODE

I ARRIVED IN Seattle in 1966 with high hopes of opening a sushi bar. I spoke next to no English, but I was filled with a sense of adventure. This is what my father had talked about. One of his children had made it to the US. Now I had to show that I could be a success here.

At the time, I was a wide-eyed twenty-five-year-old ready to experience everything I could about this country I had chosen to live in. I remember vividly the Tanakas picking me up at the airport and taking me to the Jackson Café on Jackson Street in Seattle's International District. There I tasted my first-ever serving of apple pie à la mode, and it was the most delicious thing I had ever tasted. To this day — even after all the mouthwatering salmon and oysters and matsutake mushrooms and Dungeness crab I've had — that plate of warm apple pie with a scoop of ice cream melting over it conjures up feelings of being in America like no other meal. Here's what I told the *Seattle Times*' Nancy Leson about it back in 2001:

> It was a small café that I used to go to when I first moved here. They served traditional American food like oxtail. I miss it because it was the first place I ever ate apple pie à la mode — I'd never had that kind of thing before. I still remember that taste!

A couple of hours after I finished my apple pie, the Tanakas put me to work. It was clear that I was not on vacation! Still, I had no complaints. I was too excited to rest anyway. It was my first day in a foreign country.

OPPOSITE TOP

Jackson Street in Seattle's International District. The Jackson Café can be seen on the right.

OPPOSITE BOTTOM

This photo was taken in the 1950s, directly in front of what would eventually be Tanaka Restaurant. The Bush Hotel (visible in the background) was my home for the first several months after my arrival.

Tanaka Restaurant

The clientele at Tanaka was mostly Japanese, Japanese Americans and some businesspeople who had developed a taste for Japanese food on their travels. I was surprised to see that almost no one ate raw fish. Even the Japanese Americans didn't seem to care for it. There was very little sushi being served, at least sushi like we serve on the Ginza. The Japanese Americans favored *futomaki* rolls and rice balls. There was still a stigma to eating raw fish, as if it would make you keel over in pain after a bite or two.

Now don't get me wrong: Futomaki rolls are a wonderful part of the sushi universe. These thick rolls are loved in Japan and are still consumed regularly at festive occasions. The traditional futomaki roll typically includes *tamagoyaki* (a Japanese-style omelette), cooked spinach, shiitake mushrooms, gourd shavings, fish powder and other ingredients. It's thick enough to be difficult to roll without having the innards bursting out, so it's no easy feat for a chef to prepare, and it's tasty and nutritious. The thing is that futomaki is just one sliver of the sushi world in Japan, but in late 1960s Seattle, it accounted for most of the sushi being consumed.

I'd say five percent or less of the sushi I served in those first months at Tanaka was the type of sushi I prepared in Tokyo. If a customer had a request, it was typically for a fusion-type roll. I realized that my dream of creating the

OPPOSITE & ABOVE
My workplace, the Tanaka Restaurant.

DIRECTLY ABOVE
A Japanese restaurant sign advertising tempura and sukiyaki. Sushi had yet to catch on.

I often catered special events in the Seattle area. The opposite upper left photo and the top photo on this page show me serving sushi at an event for the Nomura Kyogen group held at local sculptor and painter George Tsutakawa's home in 1968.

first full-service sushi bar in the area was going to take some time. But that was OK with me. After all, I had just spent six years of my life as an apprentice, so patience was not a problem.

I learned during my apprenticeship that it's a chef's role to teach his customers about the cuisine he's serving. If I did my job right, more and more customers would want to try sushi as it is served on the Ginza, I thought.

I also started to realize how much I would have to work with. I would walk along Pike Place Market and see the plentiful salmon and Dungeness crab. Vendors would crack open the crabs and wash away the orange guts, which always seemed like such a waste to me. Those guts can go into miso soup, giving it a zesty kick. There were Manila clams, just like back home in Japan. The rumor was that those exquisitely designed clams had hitched a ride on freighters long ago and found the Puget Sound to their liking. These clams are more oblong and intricate in their design than the plentiful butter clams. The Manila clams are far more tasty, too. It was good to see them in the neighborhood.

The Sound was full of rockfish too, and we could serve it all year long because the water stayed cold enough. The cold water also meant the fish were chockful of omega 3 fatty acids.

Some people may turn up their nose at pulling fish out of the Sound, but back then, the water was far cleaner and

no one hesitated to eat what they could catch. You could go down to the beach for a clam dig, hook a rockfish, dig for a geoduck, and no one worried about mercury content or toxins. Today's Sound is far more fragile. We need to take care of her.

Seattle has it all: the mountains, the water and the vibrant Pike Place Market.

We also got halibut from Alaska, which is good almost all year round. And spot prawns, which are their tastiest in the spring and summer.

I found as I started to explore this region that the Cascades hid a treasure trove of matsutake mushrooms, and that Shilshole Bay was filled with delicious varieties of kelp. At low tide, you could pull all sorts of seaweed from the water.

In short, as I began to explore Seattle and its environs, it dawned on me that the region was blessed with a natural bounty.

During those first few years in Seattle, my mind began to grasp certain truths about my new home that would help me in business later. In those days, the waters were teeming with fresh seafood; there was no need to fly in expensive imports if I could figure out good combinations of local fish to serve. Plus, the locals had certain habits that presented an opportunity to me, like the throwing away of perfectly good

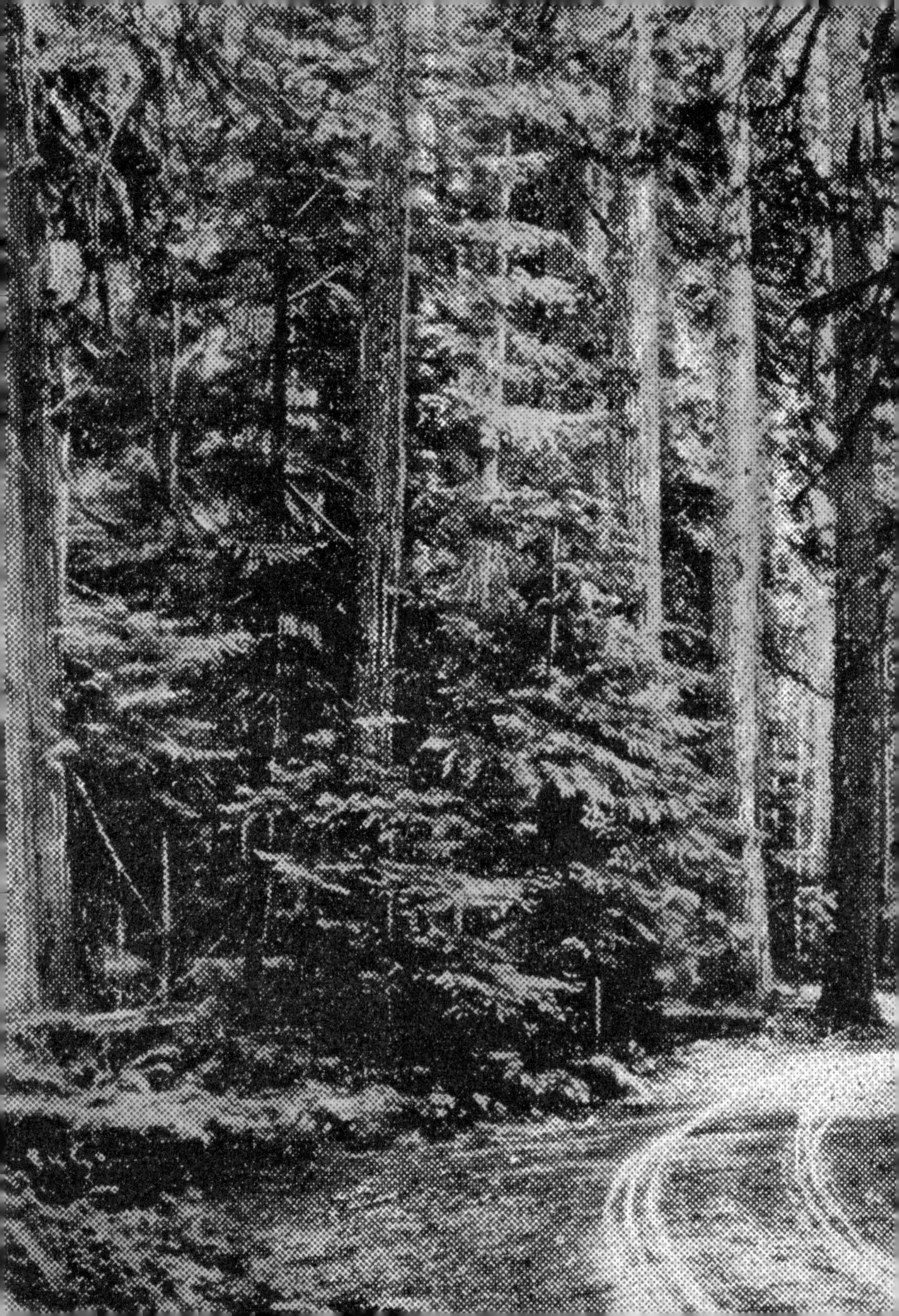

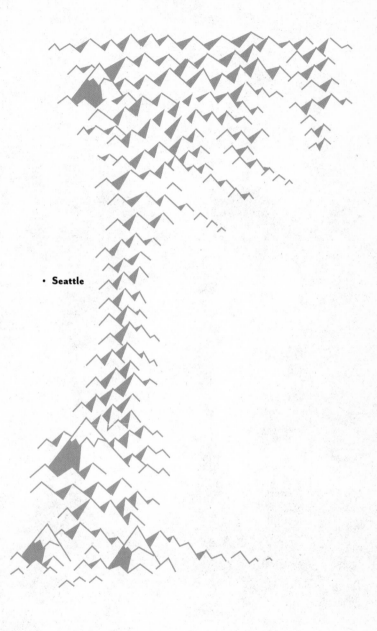

• Seattle

Dungeness crab guts. The American penchant for entre-
preneurialism must have been rubbing off on me, because I
started to see ways that I could differentiate my cuisine from
the other Japanese fare. But I was young, inexperienced and
indebted to the Tanakas. For now, I would bide my time and
do my job as well as possible.

I would also start to find more to like about life in Seattle. At the time, I was on a student visa. I used to call it my
"stupid" visa, because I was a horrible student, but it was the
one way I could live in the US at the time, so I begrudgingly
went to classes at Seattle Community College. One class that
was a lot of fun was a cake-decoration class, where I learned
how to decorate those delicious American-style cakes and
all sorts of other items. I was the only male in the class. And
there was one student, Ritsuko, also from Japan, who caught
my eye.

It seems that I caught hers too. We dated and soon found
ourselves in love. We were both expats living far from home,

which is a romantic notion that probably helped draw us together. Plus, being the only man in the class, I had little competition! We both had deep ties to our home country — me with my sushi, Ricky with her *shodo*, or calligraphy, which adorns the walls of Shiro's in Belltown today and the pages of this book. I think our passions for sushi and shodo helped keep us grounded as we dated, fell in love, got married and raised a family in a foreign land. We never felt too disconnected from Japan.

After dating for a few years, we were married in a small ceremony in Seattle in 1970. I think I can safely say that I was the first Japanese immigrant — heck, I was probably one of the first men in the history of humankind — to make his own wedding cake.

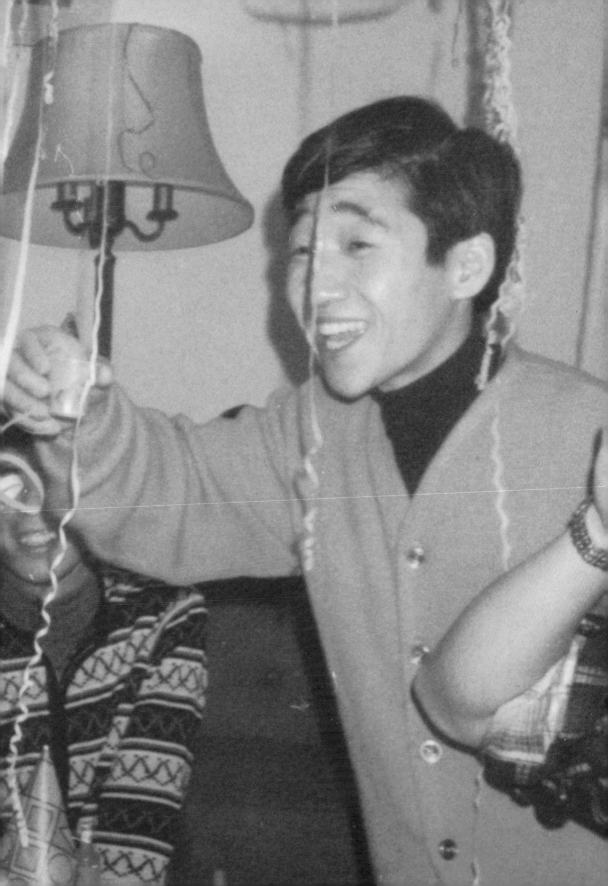

CHAPTER SIX

BUCKETS OF ROE

BEING FROM JAPAN, I saw life in Seattle through a different lens than my American friends, and I realized early on that this gave me a certain advantage. In other words, I saw treasure where others saw trash.

Case in point: during my early years in Seattle, I would walk the fishing piers, admiring the beautiful fish that had been caught. But I noticed, to my shock and dismay, that the fishermen would clean their salmon and dump all the roe out into buckets, to be thrown out or used for bait later. This sushi staple — the eggs that make *ikura* — was of practically no value to them.

Today, even the novice sushi fan knows the pleasures of ikura. But back then, it was just thought of as bait or waste.

The Japanese word "ikura" comes from the Russian word for caviar, *ikra*. Of course, the traditional Russian caviar is not salmon roe, but the roe of Beluga sturgeon. Salmon roe is prized by Eskimos for its health benefits. The eggs are said to be exceptionally high in omega 3 fatty acids, which are good for your brain and heart, but they're also high in sodium, which is not. Some researchers even say that roe can help reduce depression.

We know this now, but back in the late 1960s and early 1970s when I was walking the fishing piers and markets of Seattle, the Americans saw the gelatinous orange little balls as bait, and the Japanese saw it as a tasty delicacy atop vinegared rice wrapped in seaweed. That's all it was. Nobody thought about its health benefits back then.

But I could see that the fishermen of Seattle had more roe

Salmon fishing out of Westport on Washington's Pacific coast.

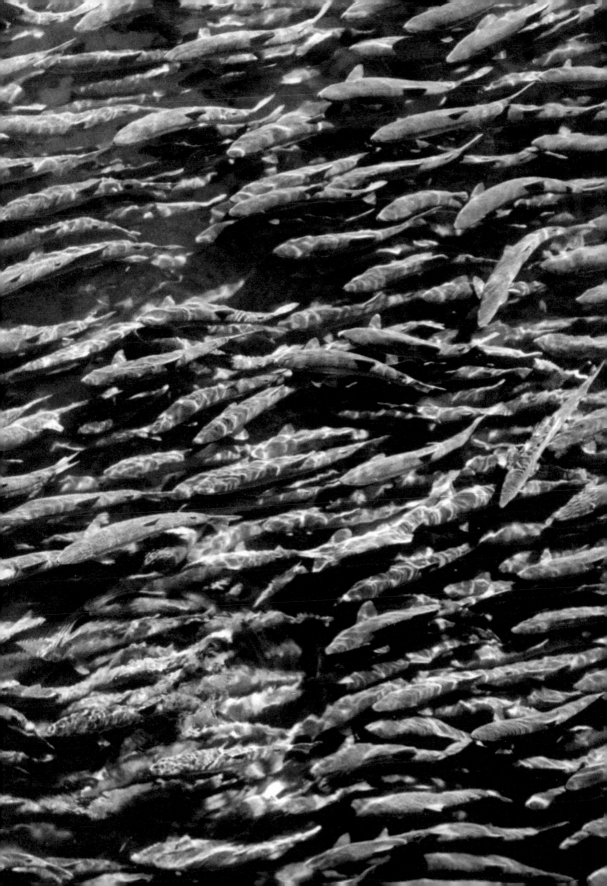

than they knew what to do with. Once they put aside some for bait, the rest would be washed away. So I devised a plan: I would walk the piers, talk to the fishermen, let them get to know me, then ask if I could take their excess roe. I would empty out their buckets, clean, rinse and return them, then take my newly filled buckets of roe back to the restaurant to make the freshest pieces of ikura in the Northwest.

And think of the profit margins on those pieces of sushi! I had paid nothing for the most expensive ingredient!

Before you start thinking I am a cheapskate (and believe me, I have been called worse), let me make clear that the bottom line is not always on my mind. While I usually stick to the maxim that "cheapest is best" because "cheapest" means local and fresh and less money and time spent on transportation, there are certain ingredients that are worth spending more on. One of those items is seaweed, or *nori*, as it's known in Japan. There's no sense skimping when it comes to nori. Anyone who's expectantly bit into a piece of sushi only to find that the nori is soggy and chewy knows what I'm talking about. Good, crisp nori is key, and that's why I say it's worth it to spend more on seaweed.

While we're on the topic, sheets of nori should be roasted only on one side. The trick I use is to take out two sheets of nori, hold them back to back, and wave them over an open flame. That ensures that only one side gets roasted. Then, whenever possible, serve it right away. The crisp, roasted nori is the most flavorful and delivers a satisfying crunch.

Now that everyone is on to the delicious taste and health benefits of salmon roe, I can no longer get free buckets of

the stuff down at the pier. Now I pay for the eggs just like anyone else. But my approach to shopping — looking for the competitive advantage by going against the grain — hasn't changed. For example, in recent years, when I'd go to buy salmon from one of the local dealers, I noticed that a lot of the salmon was cleaned and filleted for customers who didn't want to do the knifework themselves. I asked one of my favorite stores what it did with the salmon skin. We throw it away, came the reply.

I asked them to save me the skin from the best-looking salmon. I would come around and collect it when I did my shopping there, then I would bring the skin back to the restaurant and create our beloved salmon skin salad, which features broiled salmon skin in sweet rice vinegar. A lot of my American customers say the roasted skin tastes like bacon!

IN THE EARLY 70s, when I was walking the fishing piers and markets and dreaming of opening a sushi bar in Seattle, the Tanaka Restaurant was struck with tragedy. Ted Tanaka was killed in a car crash. It was a sad time for all of us — after all, he was the reason I was living in the United States. His widow vowed to carry on the restaurant, and for a few months, we tried, but with him gone, it never felt right. Eventually, she decided that the only option left was to close down, and so, my first job in the United States was over.

I am forever indebted to the Tanaka family. They gave me my start in the US. It was with sadness that I left that job. But

A wedding party at Maneki,
photographed by Elmer
Ogawa in the 1950s.

I was lucky. Seattle was beginning to awaken to the charms of Japanese cuisine, and it wasn't hard to find a new job. After taking a few months off to decompress, I began working at Maneki Restaurant. That was 1970, and Maneki is still going strong today on Sixth Ave. in Seattle's International District. It's a cultural landmark.

Although my tenure there was brief, it turned out to be a seminal time for me. This fabulous restaurant gave me the opportunity to do what I couldn't quite pull off with the Tanakas. They let me operate a full-service sushi bar — Seattle's first — in the front of the restaurant. It's still there today; when you enter the restaurant, turn left and you'll find the cozy bar. This is where sushi started in Seattle.

Maneki is a culinary and cultural institution in Seattle. It opened in 1904 and presided over Seattle's thriving Nihonmachi for decades. The original restaurant was a huge place, nicknamed "The Castle." It could seat five hundred people. But when the internment came and all the Japanese and Japanese Americans running the place were carted off to Minidoka, the restaurant was ransacked and left in ruins.

Once the war ended and the Japanese Americans were let out of the camps, a group resurrected Maneki in a building next to the original. It is a smaller place, more intimate than The Castle, with private tatami-mat rooms and quiet bars in the front and back. Today, the restaurant is run by Jean Nakayama. Her late husband, Kozo, took over the restaurant from Shizuko Ichikawa, who I worked under.

In 1972, I took the big jump that my career had been slowly building up to ever since I got on that train in Kyoto and headed to the Ginza to become a sushi apprentice. I left Maneki and opened my own restaurant, the Nikko. It was at 1306 S. King St. near Rainier Ave. The space featured twelve tatami-mat rooms and, of course, a full-service sushi bar.

I had been groomed by master chefs at Yoshino, then mentored in America by the Tanakas and Shizuko Ichikawa, the previous owner of Maneki. Now my partner Shunichi Inoue and I would be running our own restaurant — I had realized my dream. But now came the hard part.

Aerial views of Seattle's International
District, 1969

❶ **Tanaka Restaurant**, 516 South Jackson Street
❷ **Maneki Restaurant**, 304 Sixth Avenue South

INTERSTATE FIVE

SOUTH JACKSON STREET

SIXTH AVENUE SOUTH

N

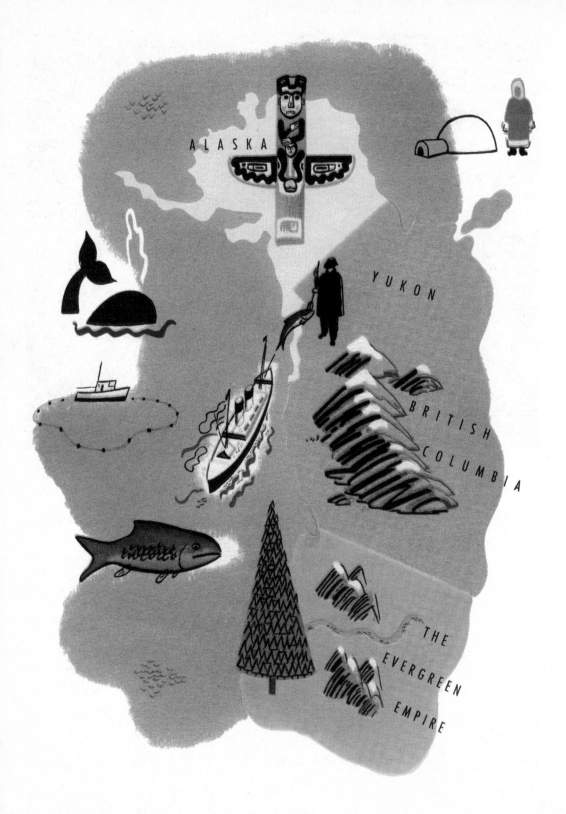

CHAPTER SEVEN

GEODUCK ON

THE BEACH

SUSHI CHEFS NEED to be good shoppers. I learned this at Tsukiji Fish Market with the chefs of Yoshino. But when I began to run my own restaurant, shopping became my obsession.

With sushi, perhaps more than any other cuisine, good shopping instincts are essential. After all, the cuisine is simple. If the ingredients are subpar, there's little you can do to hide it, especially if you're not using mayonnaise and avocado and all sorts of spicy sauces like a lot of the fusion places do. I've always been a traditionalist when it comes to sushi, so I wasn't about to hide inferior cuts of fish in sauces and spices. The fish has to be good.

If I'm going out to a sushi dinner, I'll look for a place with lots of customers. That may sound like obvious advice, but with sushi it's important: A busy restaurant will use its supply of fish faster and replenish it faster. You're more likely to be eating fresh fish. If you've ever been to a convey-or-belt sushi restaurant, you know what I mean — you want those pieces that have just been placed on the belt, not the ones that keep going round and round.

I became obsessed with ways to bring that authentic Edomae sushi tradition to Seattle, but still make it fit the city. If I flew everything in from Tsukiji, I'd quickly go broke. A single bluefin tuna might cost twenty thousand dollars. I needed to infuse my shopping with the logic of the original Edomae: Find the best-tasting fish in the Pacific Northwest's surrounding waters.

I talk a lot about local seafood in this book, but let me be clear about how I define "local." Coming from Japan, my

sense of what is local here might be a bit broader than some. I see the waters extending down through Oregon and up to Alaska as making up the Pacific Northwest. These waters provide fresh fish to markets in Seattle without relying on air freight. Most of the fish gets brought in by boat. Some of the fish can be bought straight from the boat. So to me, even a salmon from Alaska is local to the Seattle market. That's my definition anyway, and that region was in my head as I began to plan my menu. What would my standard sushi look like?

Salmon was a no-brainer. Everyone knows the Pacific Northwest has wonderful salmon. And halibut. We would have to have spotted prawns too — they're delicious here. And red snapper. And, of course, Dungeness crab. The albacore tuna, too, which makes a nice replacement for the pricey bluefin.

The smaller fish were plentiful too. The region's sardines were especially tasty. The Sound was teeming with delicious fish back then.

But if you wanted something truly exotic — exotic and local — you had to turn to the geoduck (pronounced gooey duck), the largest burrowing clam in the world. It burrows into the sand at the rate of about one inch a year, gets about three or four inches in, then settles in for one hundred years or more! The geoduck is one of the longest-living creatures on Earth, living almost a century and a half.

The geoduck of this region were like nothing I had ever seen in Japan. They are huge, even monstruous! And kind of grotesque. Back then, they were plentiful because chefs didn't know what to do with them. There were so many of them, they would lie on the beach unwanted.

I never met a fish I didn't want to taste. And when I first saw the giant geoduck, I knew I had to get it in the kitchen and see what I could do with it.

When I went to the Puget Sound beaches back in the 1970s, you could dig three inches or so and find a healthy geoduck. They were everywhere. Today, that approach won't work. The geoduck has become a hot export, especially to China, and professionals will use vacuum tubes to reach much farther into the sand and find the geoduck still burrowed in there.

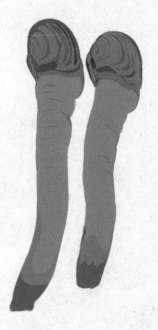

When I first arrived here, I couldn't even find geoduck in the stores. When sushi was barely catching on in the 1980s, I could get it for eighty-nine cents per pound. Today, after the sushi explosion and the rise of the Chinese middle class, it's more like eighteen to twenty dollars a pound. I fear for the geoduck — it's being overconsumed and has a high price on its head.

And I suppose in some way, I am responsible. Back in the 1970s, I went clamming a lot along the Puget Sound. I experimented with the geoduck and found its flesh tasty and not overly chewy. In fact, it could be exceptionally tender — and that's probably because we could literally go to the beach, get our geoduck, head back to the kitchen in less than an hour and start preparing. No refrigerated truck, no overnight stay in a warehouse, no sitting on the supermarket shelves. These giant clams were as fresh as you could get.

I believe I was the first person to serve this giant clam raw as sushi. I still serve it that way today when I can afford it. I also fried it lightly in butter. Delicious! I knew I had found a local treasure, and now I guess everybody knows.

Today at Shiro's, I serve a dish called Dynamite that includes a tender slice of geoduck with a dab of mayonnaise, mushrooms and onion sauce. I also serve Geoduck Butter Yaki in which the giant clam is cooked with shiitake mushrooms and served with asparagus, all sauteed in butter. And of course, I serve it as sushi.

The geoduck belongs in my Puget Sound version of Edo-mae sushi, as does the sea urchin, or *uni*, another exotic-looking creature that makes its home in the Pacific Northwest but is much more familiar to the Japanese than the awe-inspiring geoduck. A friend on a trip through the San Juans once told me he saw crows picking up the sea urchins in their beaks, flying up in the air with them, then dropping them on the rocks below in hopes of cracking them open and having a feast. San Juan crows have a pretty good life, I would say.

Some of the freshest, most mouthwatering sea urchins can be had in these parts. I think they are better than the uni found in Japan. These spiky little creatures live along the coast. You can find them in the intertidal waters. Sea otters

OPPOSITE

Gathering oysters at Hood Canal on Washington's Olympic Peninsula. In the bottom photo, Edwin is to my right and Ricky is to my left.

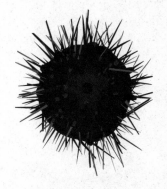

love uni as much as sushi aficionados do, so we have some competition.

But I must say that not everyone takes to uni. Even in Japan, there are those who turn up their noses at the treat. In the US, some people won't even try it — its name and its mushy consistency are enough to scare them off.

I pity these people. Uni may be an acquired taste, but once you've acquired it, there's no turning back. Plenty of my regular customers say uni sushi is their favorite.

To get people to try the local sea urchin, I often serve it *temaki* style. This is a friendlier way to try exotic-sounding seafood. "*Te*" means "hand" in Japanese, and "*maki*" means "roll," so temaki-style sushi is hand-rolled. But more importantly, it's supposed to be handed directly to the customer across the sushi counter. This is the ideal way to eat it. Obviously, we can't do this for everyone, so some temaki gets put on a plate and served the Western way. When you're able to grab a seat at the counter, you'll get it served as it is in Japan — from the chef's hand to yours.

In the US, we shape the seaweed in temaki sushi like a cone sometimes, which makes it easy to eat with your hands. In Japan, the nori is typically rounded and open at both ends.

I serve other fish temaki style to get Americans to try them. For example, *saba*, the Norwegian mackerel, is often considered too fishy for American tastes. But in Japan, it's one of our favorites, especially grilled. I created the Shiro Roll to counter some of that fishiness and get my American patrons to give it a try. The temaki roll has Norwegian mackerel (which is fattier than mackerel from California waters), shiso and ginger in a nori wrap. I add a little roasted sesame too. It's one of our best sellers.

My preference for Norwegian mackerel over the more indigenous mackerel caught off the coast of California brings up an interesting point: Going local has its limits. Sometimes, local ingredients just aren't as good, and an import is required. But the mackerel travels well and is affordable, so I felt I needed to serve it at my restaurants.

While I'm at it, let me contradict myself once more: I have said repeatedly that simple is best with sushi. I'm a

traditionalist. However, I see some chefs doing interesting things with fusion, and I've tried to do them from time to time as well. There's no sense being thick-headed about it. There may very well be a few fusion dishes out there that are just as good as the simple sushi.

Perhaps the most experimental sushi I've created is Shiro's Wrap. I was in LA years ago, and I dined on sushi made with a soybean wrap instead of nori. It's like rice paper, but it's made of soybeans. I decided to use it in Seattle, but with Northwest ingredients. Shiro's Wrap includes crab meat, mayonnaise and sriracha (a Thai chili sauce), which is all lightly heated and wrapped in the soybeans with some cucumber. It's the first soybean wrap I made, and it is still very popular. Some people even order it for dessert!

But back to my version of Edomae sushi in Seattle. Despite all the wonderful seafood in this area, my ultimate favorite local fish may surprise you. It's small, plentiful and often overlooked when we talk about local delicacies. My favorite Pacific Northwest fish is the ocean smelt. No fisherman ever bragged about the size of the smelt he caught, but these little fish are wonderfully versatile and tasty.

The ocean smelt is one of the most under-appreciated fish in the Pacific Northwest. Big fish companies don't even bother with it — you have to go through a couple of family businesses to buy it wholesale.

The lucky thing for the smelt is that the fisheries can't come in and scoop up too much of the fish in one go, so it doesn't seem that profitable to them. Plus it is perishable. Thus, this little fish is left to the little distributors.

Smelt is especially delicious in summer, when it reaches peak flavor. But you can find it for sale all year long.

I used to fish in the La Conner Smelt Derby Festival held in late February. The daffodils were in bloom and everyone would fish off the dock. I fell in love with the little fish back then.

It's an extremely versatile fish. In fact, I once made a ten-course dinner with smelt in every course. I recommend to some of my American friends to just fry the little fish in a pan and make a sandwich with it. Delicious!

In Japan, we have *shishamo*, a type of smelt that is sometimes translated as ocean smelt, other times as *chika*. In Seattle, it's a fish related to the shishamo and referred to as ocean smelt and sometimes surf smelt. I know it's confusing, but the smelt indigenous to the Puget Sound has a different flavor and texture from Japan's shishamo. You don't need a license to fish it. The Puget Sound still teems with them, although they are having a harder time finding places to spawn because of the rapid development of this region. They are a vital food source for our beloved salmon, and because they feed on plankton, they're low in mercury. I can't say enough about these little guys!

I believe I was the first chef to serve these fish as sushi back when I was working at Maneki in the early 1970s.

At my restaurant, I often serve them deep-fried with plum sauce and a shiso leaf. The dish is called Smelt Ume Shiso Age. But I also serve smelt broiled, marinated with sliced sweet onions, grilled with salt *shioyaki* style, as sushi on a sansho leaf and as thin slices of sashimi.

All these local ingredients inspired me as I ran Nikko. The steady flow of customers inspired me too. But none inspired me more than my first visitors on the first day of business. I opened the door at five-thirty on the very first day to find a family waiting to come in. This was a good sign, I thought. And it was — it was the beginning of a special relationship I would come to share with four generations of the Hisken family.

On that first night at Nikko, Perry Hisken brought his family, including his four grandchildren — Eric, Steve, Peter and Mary. They became regulars and we eventually became

Standing in front of the large, red *torii* gate that marked the entrance to Nikko.

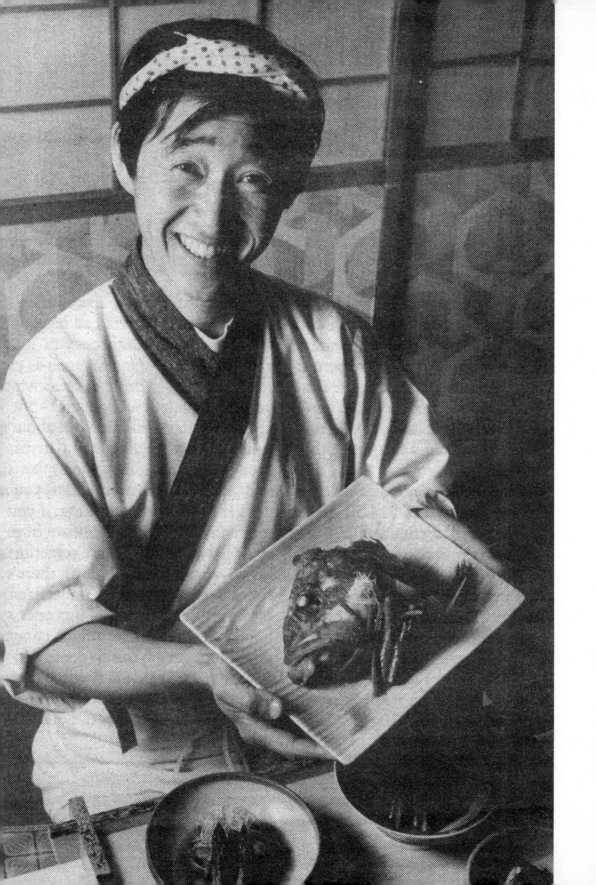

personal friends. Later, in 1986, when I opened Hana on Capitol Hill, I decided to tell them in advance, and on opening night, there they were, first in line. We repeated this ritual when I moved the Nikko to the Westin Hotel, when the whole family came, and finally, in 1994, when I opened Shiro's. Whenever I opened a new restaurant in the Seattle area, I had some members of the Hisken family be the first guests to be seated. They are my lucky charm!

Today Steve Hisken, a corporate real estate executive with Washington Partners and the grandson of Perry, brings his family to dine at Shiro's. His three children Kate, Matt and Eric are becoming sushi gourmands at a young age. They are the fourth generation of the family to enjoy my cuisine. If I'm blessed with longevity, perhaps I will meet the fifth.

The 1970s was a wonderful time for Ricky and I. We had our only child, Edwin, and Nikko became a small but successful restaurant in Seattle's International District. It was a quiet time. In some ways it was the calm before the storm of the 1980s when sushi began its expansion across the globe and Japan's economy developed an enormous bubble, leading to all sorts of money being invested in schemes and projects. Seattle was sleepier back then, too, before the Microsoft millionaires and Starbucks and Amazon. Boeing was the big business back then — Boeing and the maritime industry.

There were only a few sushi restaurants in the city even at the close of the 1970s, with Nikko and Maneki leading the charge. No one had any idea that sushi was on the verge of massive expansion. But we could see Americans slowly getting a taste for it.

The next decade would bring a lot of change. By the early 1990s, I was feeling burnt out and contemplating retirement. I look back at that first decade of Nikko restaurant as one of the happiest times of my life, and I owe much of that happiness to the support of the Japanese American community in Seattle. They have always been there for me.

FOLLOWING PAGE
Sketches from Shiro's notebooks.

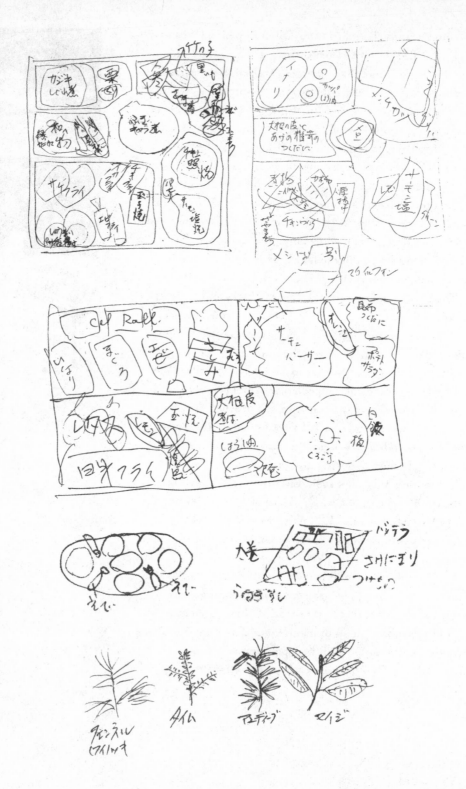

CHAPTER EIGHT
PULLING KELP,
PICKING MATSUTAKE

WASHINGTON STATE HAS so many treasures in its
midst. Japanese visitors to Seattle used to take home gifts
of Rainier cherries in boxes made of Paulownia wood. A
single cherry used to cost a dollar! The state is blessed with a
natural beauty few can match. We should never take that for
granted. As Seattle develops, we've already lost some things.
With a thriving city like Seattle, that's inevitable, but it's still
a little sad.

I remember times when you could pull beautiful bunches
of kelp out of Shilshole Bay, take it back to the kitchen and
boil it. It was fresh and delicious — nothing better.

I even hold a license for pulling kelp in this area. I'm not
sure how many people do, but it can't be many.

For this book, I went with photographer Ann Norton to
pull kelp out of that bay. It was low tide, and we walked out
on the sand until I found some particularly photogenic spot.
It brought back a flood of memories. There were still some
lovely strands of seaweed in the water, but in earlier decades
it seemed like an endless bounty. The truth is, the bounty *will*
end unless we're better stewards of the land.

When my son Edwin was old enough, we used to go
mushroom-picking in the Cascades. You could find bunches
of matsutake growing in the shade of a tree without much
problem at all. Today, friends won't even tell friends where
they pick their matsutake because the really good sources of
that delicate mushroom have dwindled.

Nothing lasts forever. As I look back on my life, I realize
how blessed I was to be a chef in the Seattle area before the
city grew up.

Once a city begins to find its economic might, a lot of things become possible, but life also gets more complicated. In the 1980s, I had a lot of opportunities. At Nikko, we prepared meals for Japan Airlines flights to Tokyo. It was a difficult, slim margin venture, but it was also very prestigious. In those days, JAL food was thought to be the best in the airline industry. I'm hoping the meals made at Nikko were part of the reason.

I also helped open a sushi bar in Capitol Hill called Hana. We had big plans back then: We were going to introduce Seattle to conveyor-belt sushi. It was the mid 1980s, which, as it turns out, was too early for the conveyor-belt idea by almost two decades. Still, once we abandoned the conveyor belt, Hana found its footing and has been going strong ever since.

I also was asked by the Westin Hotel chain to sell my restaurant and move it inside of the downtown Seattle hotel. In 1988, Aoki Corp. had bought the hotel chain. The Japanese management was looking to upgrade its restaurants, and having a Japanese restaurant in a major metropolitan hotel would be a status symbol. The Westin wanted to buy the Nikko and keep me on as head chef. I accepted the offer, and in 1992, a fancier version of my original Nikko restaurant opened in the Seattle hotel.

I soon chafed under the new management. I found myself doubting my choices and not enjoying my work. I had been my own boss for a long time, and it was hard for me to adjust to having bosses again. After a year at the Westin, I resigned.

Twenty-five years into my life in Seattle, I was without a job and without a restaurant. We had made enough money in that quarter century not to panic, but I was at loose ends. After talking with Ricky, I decided to travel and reflect on my family's future. The truth is, Seattle, I almost left you.

I found a letter I wrote to a friend in Dallas around this time that sums up my feelings then. Here it is:

U. Uguma.

非常にうれしく、又思いがけない年賀状をいただき心よ
り申し上げます。ダラスのリミアトに□みえて、全て□甘そ
に飛んでいたなが長□姿を思い出すと自分自身も何んだか元気
ファイトが出る
ごが身を 過去2年間いろいろな人生経験をいたしま
　　　　　　　　自分の夢を追求するべく
ず　日光レストランを売りました。今 Westin Hotel のオーナーで
　　番不□数に
トランをミートルWestin Hotel 内に移し私が □日光レストランが
作りましたが、庸われ社長は私に合め□□取を託しました
□身の社会勉強をすべく、自由の身となり、□□□□□□□□

□□□どの様な可能性があるのかを見るべく、いろいろな所を
一番に訪れたのがベトナムでした。去年の1月から2月に
□□して、日本レストラン（3軒ありましたが市市□の□にあたに□
□□□□□□が□□□□□）世市内の□□□様→を歩る
物価の豊富に喜こびを感じる半面、日本レストランの□□
　　　　　　　　　　現□は知りませんが 自□
□□にはつくづくこ□ではいけないと□痛感致し、久保田
□そうになった時にいろいろとか話を致しました。その時は自分□は
□□□麗し考え商工会議所の□日本語の上手な方と会って
ました□余りに、国□に対する知識が□□すぎる主見って
　　べんた

January 1994

Azuma-san,

Your New Year's postcard was a joy to receive. Thank
you. I fondly recalled the time you flew in from
Dallas, and drank and ate and had a good time with me.
The enthusiasm you showed during that time gave me
strength too.

In the last two years, I've had all sorts of life
experiences as I follow my dreams (maybe that's a
bit of an exaggeration). First, I sold the Nikko
restaurant. The owner of the Westin Hotel, Aoki Corp.,
bought it and moved it inside the hotel. I was in
charge of the restaurant for a year, but the president
and I didn't get along, so I resigned. During the past
year, I traveled all over to study the world and think
about my and my family's future. I went on a lot of
trips to check out various possibilities.

First, I traveled to Vietnam. I spent about a week
there from late January to early February. I found
three Japanese restaurants and went to one near
city hall. I was impressed with the seafood and the
agricultural bounty, but - I'm not sure if it is
still like this - the prices were quite high and the
restaurant was of a poor quality. It just wasn't right.
When I met with Consul-General Kubota for a meal, I
talked to him about this.

At the time, I was free, so I thought about working
as a restaurant manager. I spoke with someone at the
Chamber of Commerce who spoke good Japanese. But in the
end, I felt that I lacked sufficient knowledge about the
country, and with some regrets decided to back away
from the idea.

It may be too late, but Vietnam still lingers in
my mind.

After that, I traveled and walked around places in the
United States, Europe, Central and South America. I
noticed the cultural and ethnic differences and how
Japanese restaurants were interpreted in each place. It
was very interesting.

It was a valuable 1993. I realized I still have
something in me. I gained some confidence. That's where
I am today.

Now I'm in Shimotakaido in Tokyo, where I've been
helping open and manage a restaurant for a person who
had been a customer of mine in Seattle for twenty
years. I've lived in Tokyo for three months. Working
every day, I'm reminded of how difficult conducting
business in Tokyo is.

My life in Tokyo has served as a stimulating time.
I've filled some voids in me after twenty-five years in
America. But I've made up my mind to stop working here
in February. My plans for the future are being laid
right now. If you're still going to Vietnam, I'd like
to visit again as well.

Sincerely,
Shiro

ABOVE
Visiting the Tsukiji Fish Market
in Tokyo.

OPPOSITE
In Ho Chi Minh City, Vietnam.

CHAPTER NINE

KANSHA

VIETNAM WAS ON my mind, but Ricky and Edwin were
waiting for me back in Seattle. When I returned from Tokyo
in early 1994, I felt refreshed from my travels and ready to
work again. I had been on the road more or less for a year. I
had sorted out my thoughts and realized there was much left
for me to do. It was time to settle down and get cooking.

Deep down, despite my flirtation with Vietnam, I knew
Seattle was the place to make my next restaurant. I had
worked in the International District, Capitol Hill and
downtown, but where should I go next? It was my son, then
a young man, who told me, "Dad, go to Belltown."

In the 1980s and 90s, Belltown was kind of sleepy. There
wasn't much going on — a few clubs, a couple of restaurants.
Or at least that's how it appeared to a Japanese man in his
fifties. But Edwin was tapped into the youthful vibe of the
neighborhood. Belltown was transforming into a more up-
scale version of Pioneer Square. He could tell that it was
turning into a nightlife hub beyond bars and clubs. I'm glad
I listened to him.

I rented a space at 2401 Second Ave. in 1994 and opened
Shiro's. I was practically in the shadow of the Westin. The
Hiskens were there to launch my new restaurant, and others
soon followed. People expressed their gratitude that I was
back in business. I was deeply touched, especially after the
year or so of travel and self-exploration I had gone through.
This was indeed home.

Over the years, I've had so many good memories in this
place. I remember the time a family came in and sat at the
counter. I was preparing some spot prawns — it was sum-

Kansha.
Calligraphy by Ritsuko
Kashiba.

OPPOSITE
Ritsuko's calligraphy adorns
the walls of Shiro's.

Tanaka RESTAURANT

1

TANAKA

516 South Jackson Street

1966-1970

MANEKI SUKIYAKI

2

MANEKI

304 Sixth Avenue South

1970-1972

Nikko Restaurant

3

NIKKO

1306 South King Street

1972-1992

Ha Na RESTAURANT

4

HANA

219 Broadway East

1986

NIKKO RESTAURANT

5

NIKKO (WESTIN)

1900 Fifth Avenue

1992

Shiro's Sushi

6

SHIRO'S

2401 Second Avenue

1995 - PRESENT

mer, and those prawns are at their peak flavor then — and I often liked to let the prawns jump around a little for the spectacle of it. Then I would chop off their heads and prepare the sushi. The little girl and boy looked horrified. The boy said in a very stern voice, "Hey, don't do that!" I made a mental note never to prepare live spot prawns in front of children again.

I remember catering the World Trade Organization meeting in 1999 just as all hell was breaking loose in the streets. I remember in the 70s serving a thin, bespectacled computer programmer at the old Nikko sushi bar. This smiling computer programmer would become one of the most successful and wealthy men on Earth. I am still honored to cater for Bill and Melinda Gates every year at their annual CEO summit at their beautiful home. I remember when a new baseball sensation from Japan came to Shiro's for the first time. And it's still a thrill to serve Ichiro when he pops in from time to time during the off-season.

5/16/07
Bill Gates
House

I am humbled to call former Seattle Symphony Music Director Gerard Schwarz a regular customer. In fact, he once brought his wife and two children to the restaurant along with two avocados. He knows I don't do fusion much, but his kids weren't big traditional sushi fans. I was more than happy to prepare an avocado roll for them!

But the most touching memories for me have nothing to do with famous people. My joy is in being able to share Japanese culture with everyone.

I remember catering a man's seventieth birthday party in Magnolia. Just about everyone was Caucasian, and the only food being served was sushi. It was a spine-tingling moment for me. I was part of a new era!

If I would have remained in Japan and opened up a restaurant in Tokyo, I would've just been one of thousands. It is because of Seattle that I have been blessed with experiences beyond my wildest dreams.

As sushi has gone global, it has become part of many traditions. I've catered bar mitzvahs, birthday parties, corporate outings, anniversaries, wedding receptions. Sushi has become as American as — dare I say it — apple pie.

I recently read in the newspaper the results of a poll

taken of foreign visitors to Japan. They were asked at Narita Airport to name their favorite things about Japan. First was "food." Second were the *onsen* hot springs. Their favorite foods? Sushi, ramen and sashimi, in that order. The tastes of the world have changed.

I'm happy to in some small way be a part of this change. But I'm also worried about the future. We need to be more sensitive about the environment for fish, or they will disappear. *Hamachi*, *maguro*, *tai* (snapper) — there are fewer and fewer wild fish these days. More fish are coming from farms. You can change the taste of the farmed fish depending on what you feed them. It's scary. The effects aren't seen right away. It takes time. I do worry about this.

But more than anything else I am grateful. There is a Japanese word for gratitude that is pronounced "*kansha*." That is the word I would like to offer to the people of Seattle and all my guests from out of town. *Kansha shiteimasu*. I am forever grateful for your support.

Now that I'm seventy, people ask me when I will retire. Retire? I haven't thought about it. I have been very lucky. I can talk directly with guests and tell them about the seafood. I'd like to continue this as long as I can. I like to work together with young people. Without work, I'd have nothing to do. I can travel once in awhile, but work is fun.

In 2007, I sold all but a minority interest in my restaurant to Yoshi Yokoyama, founder of I Love Sushi, and another investor. This move relieved me of the day-to-day financial responsibilities and allowed me to concentrate on what I do best: shop, prepare and cook. And banter with the guests. Being a sushi chef is like being a chef and a bartender at the same time. I guess I'm a "sushi bartender."

I hope that the legacy of Edomae sushi can live and grow in the Pacific Northwest. As sushi goes global, it also needs to go more local. We lose something when sushi becomes nothing more than nutritious fast food. Savor every bite, every minute.

I hope that long after I'm gone, traditional sushi will find a way to adapt to different regions of the world. With smart stewardship and respect for the oceans, the Pacific Northwest can remain a paradise for sushi lovers.

A DAY IN THE LIFE OF
SHIRO KASHIBA

09:00   Shiro wakes up.

10:00   Shiro has a "brunch" of rice, *tsukemono* (pickled vegetables) and miso soup with green onions and tofu. "I've been eating that breakfast for thirty-five years. I've never had a sick day. The only time I feel bad is when I have a hangover."

13:00   Arrive at the restaurant. Check reservations and supplies.

13:30   Meet with the servers, kitchen staff and chefs. Head out with some of the staff to go shopping. "Once I smell the fish, I get excited about work."

14:30   Return from first round of shopping and drop off material. Then head to the International District and drop in on three or four places. This is where he looks for geoduck, abalone, oysters, rockfish, razor clams and spot prawns.

15:00   Return to the restaurant and meet with staff.

16:00   Have lunch with the staff. "This helps the staff train their tastebuds. We eat the parts of the fish that aren't for customers — the collar, the head, soup made from its bones. We discuss what tastes good and what doesn't."

17:00   Shiro's opens for business.

22:00   Shiro's closes. The staff makes friendly bets about how much money the restaurant brought in that day. Shiro gives them the total. Everyone cleans up.

24:00   Shiro returns home and drinks one Bud Lite that he bought at Costco before going to sleep.

1   Salmon
2   Albacore
3   Yellowtail
4   Fatty tuna
5   Tuna
6   Geoduck
7   Freshwater eel
8   Snapper
9   Sea urchin
10 Spanish mackerel
11 Scallop
12 Sweet shrimp

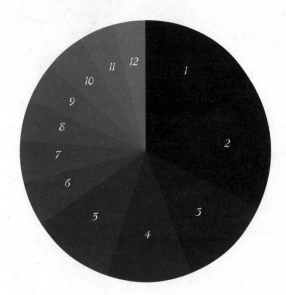

NIGIRI SUSHI SALES
ranked by popularity

1   Spicy tuna
2   Shiro's Wrap
3   Spider roll
4   Rainbow roll
5   Crab roll
6   Shiro's Roll
7   Tekka maki
8   California roll
9   Shrimp tempura

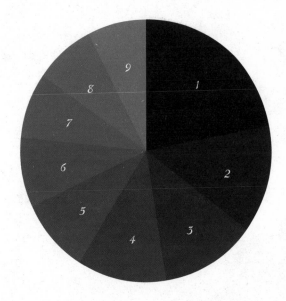

SUSHI ROLL SALES
ranked by popularity

NOTE BOOK

Made of Paper
Specially prepared in Nippon

ハイフード

Shiro

G.N &.CO   意匠登録 第3263号

**RECIPES
& TIPS**

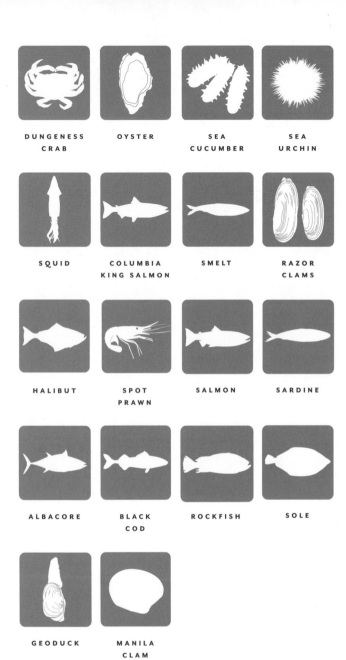

DUNGENESS
CRAB

OYSTER

SEA
CUCUMBER

SEA
URCHIN

SQUID

COLUMBIA
KING SALMON

SMELT

RAZOR
CLAMS

HALIBUT

SPOT
PRAWN

SALMON

SARDINE

ALBACORE

BLACK
COD

ROCKFISH

SOLE

GEODUCK

MANILA
CLAM

SEASONAL INGREDIENTS
SEAFOOD

Please note that availability often varies from year to year depending on
changes in weather and other factors.

	12	1	2	3	4	5	6	7	8	9	10	11

WINTER

SPRING

SUMMER

AUTUMN

KELP

FENNEL

ASPARAGUS

SANSHO
LEAF

MYOGA

MATSUTAKE

JAPANESE
EGGPLANT

CHERRY

WAPATO
TOMATO

WALLA WALLA
ONION

SEASONAL INGREDIENTS
PRODUCE

	12	1	2	3	4	5	6	7	8	9	10	11

WINTER   SPRING   SUMMER   AUTUMN

01 SHIRO'S TIPS
HOW TO COOK
SHORT-GRAIN RICE

WHAT YOU WILL NEED: a rice cooker (for 5 cups of rice, or adjust the recipe below accordingly)

Good rice is one of the key ingredients and the soul of a good Japanese meal. It requires attention to water levels and timing. New-crop rice that's just been harvested carries high levels of moisture and therefore requires less water to cook than older rice. At Shiro's, we adjust water levels to cook the rice according to the age of the rice, which can be discerned by when they are available at markets. The older the crop, the more water it requires. Here's my guideline for 5 cups of uncooked rice:

REGULAR OR MID-SEASON RICE (available at stores from April through September): Add 15% more water than the rice.

NEW RICE (January through March): Add just 10% more water than rice.

OLD RICE (October through December): Add 20% more than the rice.

- Pour 5 cups of rice into the pan of the rice cooker and fill it up halfway with water. Gently wash the rice with light circular motions with the hand. Do not squeeze or handle the rice roughly. Then rinse out the water (be careful not to let the rice out of the pot) and repeat 4-5 times until the water becomes somewhat clear. Let the rice sit for about 15 minutes until the grains absorb the water.
- Turn on the rice cooker.
- When the rice is done, let the rice sit again until the grains settle for about 15 minutes.

02 SHIRO'S TIPS
HOW TO PREPARE SUSHI RICE

One of my favorite handbooks in English, *Sushi Hygiene and Basic Techniques*, has this to say about sushi rice:

It has been said for a long time that sushi rice, or *shari*, represents sixty percent of the taste of a piece of sushi, and this is no exaggeration; the good or bad taste of sushi rests on the quality of the rice used to make it.

I agree with that statement. The quality of the rice is crucial.

INGREDIENTS (for 5 cups of rice):

3½ tablespoons sugar
1¼ tablespoons salt
½ cup rice vinegar

- Prepare rice as instructed in tip 01.
- Combine the salt and sugar with the vinegar in a bowl and mix until dissolved.
- Transfer the warm, freshly cooked rice into a large bowl, pour in the vinegar mixture and blend well in steady strokes with a large, flat spatula or spoon as if you're cutting the rice. Never pat down rice; think of it as fluffing the rice.
- Let cool to body temperature.

MACKEREL   SALMON   ABALONE   SCALLOPS   OCTOPU

KING MACKEREL   SQUID   KING MACKEREL   TUNA   YELLOWT
(SKIN SIDE)

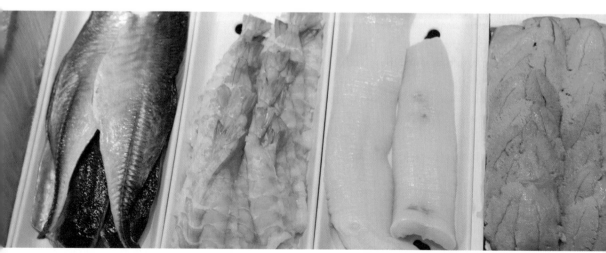

SPANISH MACKEREL   BLACK TIGER   GEODUCK   SEA URCHIN
SHRIMP

ALBACORE

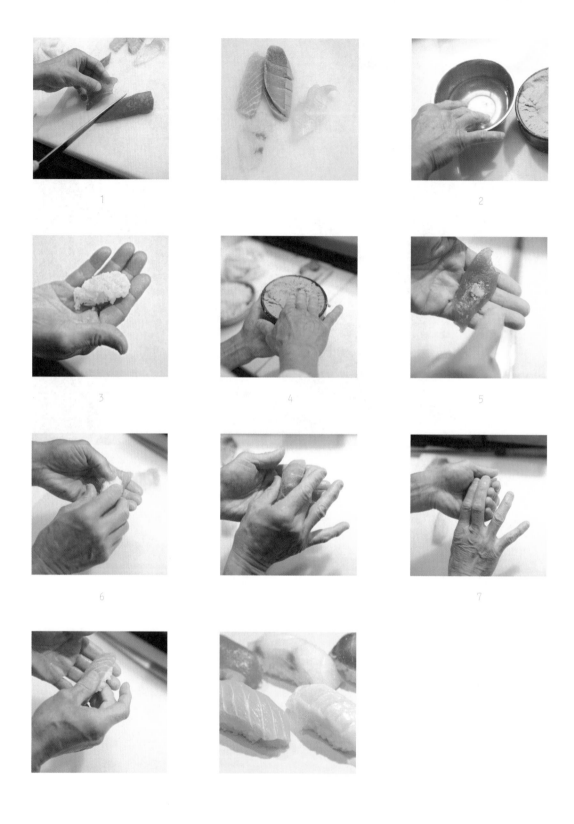

03 SHIRO'S TIPS
HOW TO MAKE
NIGIRI SUSHI

Preparing sushi is partly performance. Chefs work in front of their customers and converse with them as they work. To do this well, we need to be prepared and know where everything is. We place our knives in front of us by the cutting board, have clean and moist cloths ready for wiping down the cutting board, a container of wasabi, a bowl of *tezu*, which is the vinegary water we dip our hands into (the vinegar-to-water ratio should be the same as when making the sushi rice), and the container of sushi rice.

The fish is then brought out for slicing. If possible, use a long thin knife. In Japanese we call this a *yaginaba* knife. There are different ways to slice the fish depending on its type. For meaty fish such as albacore tuna, start with a rectangle of the flesh. Hold your knife parallel to the fish and begin slicing at a slight angle ❶. Remember to cut through the sinews, not with them. Red-fleshed fish is better in thicker cuts, so don't make the slices too thin. A typical slice should be about 3½" (about 10cm) long, 1" (about 3cm) wide and a fifth of an inch (4mm) thick.

White-fleshed fish such as smelt or mackerel needs to be thinner to bring out the best flavor and

avoid making the pieces too chewy. Place the fish skin down, and cut from the tail toward the head.

Once the *neta*, or fish topping, is prepared, dip your hand in the tezu and rub the liquid into your fingers to even it out ❷. Then scoop up enough rice for one piece of sushi ❸. This takes some practice, but as much as possible, try to grab enough rice in one scoop to avoid putting the rice back and trying again. With your other hand, pick up the neta with your thumb and index finger.

Next take the hand that has the rice in it and dip the index finger into the wasabi container ❹ and spread some wasabi on the neta ❺. Place the rice on the neta, gently curving your palm and pressing the rice with your thumb ❻.

Roll the piece of sushi down to your fingertips and press the ends of the rice with your thumb to give the piece an even shape. Then place your first two fingers of your other hand on top of the neta and press up with the hand holding the piece of sushi ❼. Now it should be ready to eat.

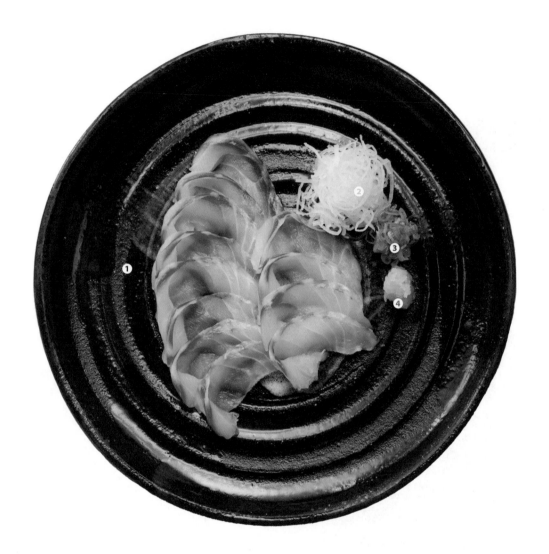

❶ Rockfish sashimi
❷ Grated daikon
❸ Green onion
❹ Momiji oroshi
❺ Ponzu sauce

04 SHIRO'S TIPS
HOW TO MAKE
SASHIMI

Preparing sashimi is very similar to preparing the
neta, or piece of fish, in sushi, but without the
application of wasabi. Use a long, thin knife, and
cut the chunk of fish at a slight angle. Remember
that red-fleshed fish such as tuna should be cut
thicker than oily white fish such as mackerel.
When slicing the fish, try not to apply uneven
pressure. That affects the taste. And cut against
the sinews, not with them. Cut quickly and
steadily. With more delicate fish, if you don't do
this, the pieces may begin to fall apart.

And always make sure your knives are as sharp as
possible. A dull blade will take the life out of the
sashimi.

Dip the slices in soy sauce with a hint of wasabi or
just apply a dab of wasabi to the fish and enjoy.

Rockfish sashimi is served
with ponzu sauce. Dip the
green onions and momiji
oroshi into the sauce
and mix.

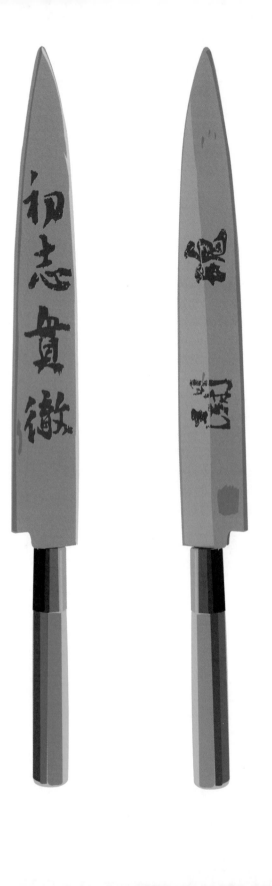

05 SHIRO'S TIPS
TOOLS OF
THE TRADE

I've been using the same knife for several decades. In fact, I have several knives that I've used for years and years. They are the sushi chef's most important tool. A typical American-made sushi knife is tapered on both sides, but the Japanese knife has teeth on only one side, making it suitable for a righty only. The flat side of a Japanese knife can be used to create better definition and a cleaner finish.

Lately, knives for lefties have appeared too, but in the old days, if you wanted to be a sushi chef, you had to learn to slice like a righty.

I sharpen my own knives on a regular basis. I care for my knives every day, and they return the favor every night at the sushi bar.

ABOVE
The grater I use for making wasabi.

OPPOSITE
Two of my favorite knives were given to me by master sushi chef Jiro Ono. My dad inscribed the cases with the following messages: (left) "Always finish what you set out to do;" (right) "Fighting spirit."

06 SHIRO'S TIPS
THE ROLE OF GINGER, WASABI, VINEGAR & GREEN TEA

Raw fish needs to be treated with respect. If it's not prepared correctly or it's not fresh, it can make you ill. The aversion to raw fish that Americans showed decades ago, when sushi was just being introduced here on a mass scale, was not unfounded. But look closer at the cuisine and you'll find that the Japanese were concerned with this issue centuries ago, and they came up with some very good ways to keep sushi healthy while enhancing its taste. The items you may take for granted when enjoying sushi — the vinegar, pickled ginger, *wasabi*, green tea and soy sauce — all play a vital role in making sure that sushi remains a healthy and delicious meal.

VINEGAR

Vinegar is an essential ingredient in sushi. After all, the word "sushi" means "vinegar rice." A sushi chef keeps a bowl of diluted vinegar, called *tezu*, nearby at all times. He constantly dips his fingers in there as he prepares pieces of sushi. The tezu solution keeps the rice from sticking when we make the sushi, but it also cleans our hands because of vinegar's wonderful antibacterial properties.

Allow me a little rant: In the US, health codes dictate that chefs wear disposable gloves while preparing sushi. I abide by these laws because I do business here, but I have to say that this way is less hygienic than the way sushi is made in Japan, with chefs constantly dipping their hands in the tezu solution. The gloves are OK for people who work in cafeterias making salads or sandwiches and things like that, but for sushi, washing your hands in the vinegar solution and using your hands to make the sushi is a cleaner way to go. But when in Rome ... I always wear my gloves. It's the law.

GARI, OR PICKLED GINGER

The pink pickled ginger that sits in a pretty pile next to your sushi is a palate cleanser. The sweet ginger is pickled in vinegar, which gives it its light pink color. The ginger has antibacterial qualities that are said to prevent food-borne illnesses, but ginger is also known for building one's immune system, improving circulation and aiding in digestion. Plus it kills the fish odor on your breath. It's an indispensable part of the cuisine.

WASABI

Wasabi, the little heap of grated green Japanese horseradish that sometimes sits on the plate, plays a vital role in killing harmful bacteria in the fish. It also kills the odor of raw fish and stimulates the appetite.

In Japan, it is assumed that the sushi one orders comes with wasabi, thus you won't see a pile of it on your plate. If you order sashimi, however, the wasabi would come with the slices of raw fish, ready for you to mix into your soy sauce. One quirk of American sushi is that the wasabi often comes on the side. I've chosen to stick with the Japanese way. Wasabi is too vital to the cuisine to leave on the side.

GREEN TEA

Green tea is often served at the end of a Japanese meal, but with sushi it is typically drunk throughout. It serves as a palate cleanser and it helps kill the smell of raw fish. It is also said to kill bacteria because of the presence of catechins, a component in green tea that has been cited as a factor in reducing body fat.

By now, you can probably sense a theme: the accompaniments to the raw fish in sushi — the vinegar, wasabi, ginger, tea and soy sauce — all help inhibit bacteria, stimulate appetite and improve your breath. The genius of sushi is that everything surrounding those succulent slabs of raw fish plays a vital — and delicious — role.

07 SHIRO'S TIPS
SOY SAUCE IS NOT
FOR DUNKING!

I don't know how many times I've had to hold my tongue behind the sushi bar when a diner soaks a piece of sushi in soy sauce as if putting a tortilla chip in a bowl of guacamole. Using too much soy sauce kills the fresh flavor of the fish and rice. Remember that sushi rice has already been seasoned. Dip the fish side of the sushi briefly in the soy sauce to enhance the flavor, not overpower it.

Also, when eating sushi, you don't need to put wasabi in the soy sauce. First-time sushi-goers might not realize this, but the sushi chef applies the wasabi when making the sushi.

This is different from sashimi, where you may want to add a hint of wasabi to your soy sauce before lightly dipping the slab of fish in.

So remember: soy sauce with sushi is not like ketchup with fries. Just a drop or so will enhance the taste. That's all you need.

08 SHIRO'S TIPS
WORDS TO USE AT THE SUSHI COUNTER

Over the years, the sushi bar has developed its own special jargon, including its very own way of counting, which allows the chef to bark out the total for a meal to the cashier without appearing rude. Here are a few of the words used by those in the know:

I used this note to memorize the sushi counting system during my days as an apprentice.

AGARI

Say *"agari"* at the end of the meal, and you'll be served a cup of green tea. The word signals that your meal is over, which is the traditional time for a hot cup of green tea to be served.

GARI

At some point long ago, sushi patrons stopped calling ginger *shoga*, the word used in Japan, and started calling it *gari*.

HIKARIMONO

Used to indicate the shiny fish such as mackerel or smelt.

MURASAKI

Those in the know may call soy sauce *shoyu*, but how many people know that the sushi-bar term for soy sauce is *murasaki*, which means "purple" and is used because of soy sauce's deep purple color?

OAISO

Check please!

SHARI

This is the word for sushi rice. Normally it is called *sushimeshi*.

09 SHIRO'S TIPS
THE IMPORTANCE OF HYGIENE

Hygiene is of the utmost importance when preparing sushi because there is always a risk that raw fish harbors bacteria and parasites which could cause foodborne illnesses. Freshwater fish is best not consumed raw. Flash freeze it first. But some saltwater fish can carry parasites too. It's important that the sushi chef and his or her staff are aware of this and do everything they can to eliminate the potential for illness. Sushi chefs carry a clean, sanitized wash cloth by their side to wipe down cutting boards constantly and keep knives clean. I recommend that you do the same if you're preparing sushi at home.

Tempura and Agemono

If you've dined at Japanese restaurants, you will know that most any seafood and vegetables can be cooked in tempura batter — shrimp, halibut, *uni*, pumpkin, carrots, onions, etc. The key to enjoying tempura is to be able to eat it right away while it's hot and crispy, right out of the kitchen. But most people can't rush out of the kitchen to sit down and eat as soon as the tempura is ready. Also, good tempura, or restaurant-grade tempura is very difficult to make. It requires very high heat, not too much oil and ice cold water. Not to mention lots of practice. Which is why tempura is a perfect meal to enjoy at a good restaurant. I have included a recipe for Smelt Ume Shiso Age, which requires tempura batter, but it doesn't require the precision and speed of a professional tempura chef.

Manila Clams Steamed with Sake

4 SERVINGS

2 lbs Manila clams

2 cups water

A pinch of salt

1 teaspoon low-sodium soy sauce

½ cup sake

½ teaspoon thinly sliced ginger

1 wedge of lemon

1-2 sprigs of sansho (optional)

The first thing you notice about the Manila clam is its beautiful shell pattern, which is more intricate than the shell of the plainer butter clam. The Manilas are also oblong, while butter clams are rounder. Manila clams are natives of Japan, but they've found a home in the Puget Sound. Some say they clung onto ships to make the trip from Japan to the US, so maybe that's why I identify with them so much! Manilas are versatile, slightly sweet and easy to cook. They have more flavor and texture and are softer than other clams. They're a favorite of mine, and I often serve them in miso soup or steamed with sake, as I describe below.

- Wash the clams in water by gently rubbing them against each other.
- Combine water with sake in a pan and cook on medium-high heat.
- Add the clams.
- Put a lid on the pan and cook until the clams open (about 3-4 minutes).
- Add soy sauce and turn off heat.
- Transfer to a bowl, add the lemon wedge and ginger before serving.
- Add a sprig or two of sansho, and enjoy.

Manila Clam Miso Soup

4 SERVINGS

16 Manila clams

3 ½ cups dashi base

4 oz red and white miso evenly
mixed

2 stalks green onion, thin sliced

Whenever possible, use Manila clams for this dish, not butter clams, which tend to be tougher and take longer to cook.

- **Pour the dashi base into a medium-size pan and cook over high heat. Stir the miso into the base using a ladle.**
- **When the miso is completely dissolved, add the Manila clams.**
- **Turn off the heat when the clams begin to open.**
- **Pour the soup into four small bowls and add the green onions.**
- **Be careful not to cook the soup too long as the clams will harden and lose their juiciness and flavor.**

Ponzu Sauce

Ponzu sauce adds a citrusy zest to a lot of Japanese dishes. When you make it from scratch, you have your choice of citrus fruits — lemon, orange or Satsuma mikan. Each will deliver the subtle zip that a good ponzu sauce needs.

I've included two versions here — one for the hard-core foodie who wants to make his or her ponzu from scratch, and one that uses store-bought ponzu for those times when you're in a hurry.

The following dishes in this book call for ponzu sauce:

- **Nabe Mono**
- **Scallops & Matsutake Broiled in Aluminum Foil**
- **Halibut Karaage**
- **Rex Sole Karaage Shiro Style**
- **Poke Belltown**
- **Salmon Skin Salad**

Of course, ponzu is a flexible sauce that can be used in all kinds of dishes, not just seafood. But it goes very, very well with most white fish.

FOODIE VERSION

For this more time-consuming version of the ponzu sauce, use the freshly squeezed juice of lemon, orange or satsuma mikan with soy sauce and mirin. Combine the mixture with *konbu dashi* or bonito-based dashi.

INGREDIENTS

- I cup freshly squeezed juice of any of the above-mentioned citrus fruit
- ¾ cup rice vinegar
- I cup and I tablespoon soy sauce
- ¼ cup mirin, cooked about 20 seconds to reduce alcohol content
- 10 grams shaved bonito
- I sheet 2½" square konbu

Combine all of the above in a bowl and let sit for 5-6 hours. Cover the mixture with linen cloth and filter into another bowl.

QUICKER VERSION

This simpler version for the busier chef can be just as tasty as the time-consuming recipe.

Combine:

I part store-bought ponzu, I part dashi base and I part soy sauce in a pan.

Add:

A fistful of dried, shaved bonito. Cook until boiling, then filter through a sieve into the pan.

Halibut Karaage with Ponzu Sauce

4 SERVINGS

2 lbs halibut filets cut into 1 ½
square inch cubes
1 cup corn starch or just enough to
lightly cover fish
5 cups vegetable oil
Salt & pepper
Lemon
Parsley

SAUCE

1 cup grated daikon radish
½ cup ponzu
⅛ cup chopped green onions

Halibut is one of the better-known fish of the Pacific Northwest. Off the coast of Alaska, you can find halibut weighing in at more than 500 pounds! The meat is slightly sweet and flaky. The citrus of the ponzu sauce plays well off the halibut. This is one of the house favorites at Shiro's.

- In a sauce pan, boil 4 cups of water with a little salt, then cook the cubed halibut for a few seconds and rinse lightly under cold water.
- Pat dry the halibut to remove the scent and lightly sprinkle salt and pepper. Let sit for about 10 minutes.
- Heat vegetable oil in a wok and wait until the internal temperature reaches about 350° F (175° C).
- Lightly cover the halibut with corn starch and fry in heated oil for 7-8 minutes.
- Put half of the sauce into a separate bowl and lightly toss with the fried halibut.
- Place the halibut in a serving dish and pour the rest of the sauce over the halibut.
- Garnish with parsley and lemon and serve.

Asparagus with Sesame Miso

4 SERVINGS

1 bunch asparagus

4 tablespoons white miso

3 tablespoons mayonnaise

½ tablespoon sesame seed paste

1 teaspoon yellow mustard

2 tablespoons mirin

2 tablespoons sugar

Asparagus grows just fine in the Pacific Northwest, although the region isn't known for it. I hear that once upon a time there was a lot of asparagus grown here. But today, it's mostly people growing it in their gardens or on small-scale lots. If you do have asparagus in your garden or at the local Farmer's Market, try this simple recipe to give the vegetable a Japanese twist.

If the ingredients sound a little unfamiliar, here are some tips: Sesame paste is available in a can or bottle at Chinese grocery stores. In Seattle, the International District south of downtown is full of wonderful Asian grocery stores. I like Lam's Seafood Market on 12th and King, and Viet Wah Supermarket on 12th and Jackson. The ID, as it is known, is a large area south of Yesler and east of 4th Ave. South.

- **Prepare a bowl of cold water and set aside.**
- **Cut off the hard part at the bottom of the asparagus stem and boil in a saucepan for a few minutes or until crisp and tender.**
- **Dip the asparagus in the bowl of cold water until properly chilled.**
- **Cut asparagus into ¾" pieces.**
- **Prepare the sauce: Mix the white miso and mirin and the remaining ingredients, including the yellow mustard, into a bowl until well blended. Then add the asparagus to the sauce and toss.**

Shiro's Special Ocean Smelt Section

If you haven't figured it out by now, I love smelt. Ocean smelt is a plentiful, versatile and surprisingly tasty little fish that is often overlooked. They are so small, you can clean them with your fingers. And they can be cooked in many different ways. I believe they are one of the greatest seafood treasures of this region.

Some people take the smelt for granted because it is small and plentiful. That's a mistake. It's lower in mercury than the bigger fish higher up the food chain and it's sustainable. So far, international markets haven't found it worth their while to start exporting the fish, which is very good news for Pacific Northwesterners. It's our local treat.

Here's what one of my regulars, Billy Brackenridge, wrote about ocean smelt at Shiro's back in 2003:

> This fish doesn't have a Japanese name because you won't find it as a sushi fish anywhere else in the world. It is a local fish that is usually fried. It only comes into season a few weeks each year. Shiro was the first and probably the only to serve it as a *hikarimono*. Hikarimono is Japanese for "something shining." Those who are "sushi *ken*," or sushi aficionados, wouldn't feel an evening of sushi could be complete without some sort of hikarimono.
>
> The smelt is very delicate, and with the skin partially peeled, it is translucent. It can be ruined with too much soy or wasabi. As the fish is so delicate, it must be served fresh, so I doubt that it will ever become popular outside of the Seattle area. I don't think it would survive freezing and shipping.

How to Clean Smelt

The main thing to remember when preparing smelt is, unless you have bought pre-cleaned smelt, you'll have to prepare them yourself. Those who fish or know how to clean bigger fish will be able to handle this with no problem. Here's what you do:

- Remove the head and guts using a knife.
- Rinse the smelt with water.
- Remove the bones by gliding the thumb between the flesh of the bones on either side of the fish. The bones should come off smoothly.

That's it. Piece of cake! But if cleaning fish is not your thing, you can find smelt that have been opened and cleaned at some local fish stores. I get mine at Mutual Fish in Seattle.

On the following pages you will find detailed illustrations on how to clean a smelt.

Use a knife to remove the head.

Slice off just enough of the belly to
remove the guts.

Rinse the smelt in lightly salted water and
toss out the guts. Make a longer incision in
the belly toward the tail

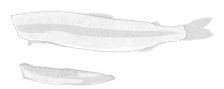

Hold the smelt with one hand and glide the
thumbnail of your other hand along the flesh
above the spine from head to tail to remove
the spine.

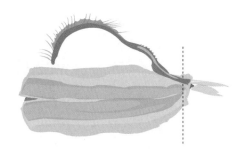

Flip the smelt over. Place your thumbnail beneath the spine and pull the smelt toward you with your other thumb to completely remove the bones.

Cut off the tail and spine.

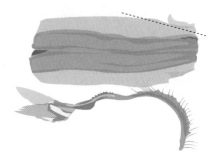

Sometimes small bones get left behind. Inspect the smelt and remove any bone remnants.

TO STORE

Sprinkle salt over a plate. Put the smelt filet on the plate and sprinkle more salt over it. Let the filet sit for 3 minutes.

Rinse the smelt filet in clean water. Place the smelt in a sieve to drain water, then store in a refrigerator.

Use the same day.

FOR SASHIMI

Peel the skin from the filets.

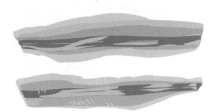

Smelt Nanbanzuke

4 SERVINGS

8 smelt
½ medium-sized onion
thinly sliced
2 stalks green onion
4 cups vegetable oil
1 lemon slice

SAUCE
Thinly sliced red pepper
2 cups water
¾ cup rice vinegar
½ cup low-sodium soy sauce
½ cup mirin

Nanbanzuke is a cooking style used with fish or meat in Japan. The word *"nanban"* means "southern barbarian," and *"zuke"* means pickled or marinated, so you can remember this dish as the Southern Barbarian Marinade. It's a lot like escabeche, and some say that Portuguese traders brought the dish to Japan hundreds of years ago. Whatever the history, we've made it our own, and cooking fish nanbanzuke style is considered traditional Japanese cuisine today.

But smelt nanbanzuke is a local treat. It's a refreshing meal when the weather turns warm.

- **Clean the smelt in lightly salted water. Remove the head and innards, rinse again in water and gently wipe off excess moisture.**
- **To prepare the sauce, combine in a pan and heat: water, rice vinegar, mirin and soy sauce and red pepper.**
- **Add vegetable oil to a wok and heat until the temperature of the oil rises to about 320° F (160° C).**
- **Lightly flour the smelt and fry them in the vegetable oil for 8-9 minutes.**
- **Add the cooked smelt to the sauce while the sauce is still hot and simmer for 30 minutes. (The smelt can be stored for 4-5 days).**

TO SERVE
Cut each cooked smelt into 2-3 pieces and layer on top thin sliced onions and green onions. Pour 3-4 tablespoons of the sauce over the smelt and onions, and garnish with a slice of lemon.

Smelt Ume Shiso Age

1 SERVING

½ cup tempura batter
(prepared according to package
instructions)
2 filets smelt sliced open
1 teaspoon ume paste
4 large shiso leaves
2 pieces of salmon sashimi
Salt and pepper
Vegetable oil for deep frying
1 lemon wedge
1 toothpick

"*Ume*" means plum in Japanese. I use a little plum paste
(which can be found at Mutual Fish and Uwajimaya in
Seattle, by the way) and shiso leaves to jazz up this deep-
fried dish. "*Age*" means fried and is pronounced "ah-
gay," so this has nothing to do with aging, just in case
you were wondering. The salmon slices tucked into the
smelt make this a Pacific Northwest delight.

- **Prepare tempura batter and set aside.**
- **Lightly sprinkle salt and pepper over each smelt.**
- **Apply a thin coat of ume paste on the smelt.**
- **Place two sheets of shiso leaves side by side on top of
  the smelt.**
- **Add the sliced salmon and roll smelt firmly around it to keep
  the salmon in place.**
- **Fasten the end of the roll with a toothpick and dip into
  tempura batter.**
- **Fry in 320° F (160° C) oil for 4-5 minutes.**

TO SERVE
**Slice into 2-3 pieces, arrange on a small plate and add a
lemon wedge.**

Fried Smelt

4 SERVINGS

8 filets smelt sliced open
1 pack panko (Japanese-style
bread crumbs)
1 cup flour
Egg mix (2 eggs, 3 tablespoons
water)
Vegetable oil for deep frying
Salt and pepper

This recipe calls for smelt, but it is also wonderful for snapper, rockfish, halibut — white fish generally used in fish and chips — as well as salmon. One of my favorite meals of all time is a fried smelt and vegetable sandwich.

- **Lightly sprinkle salt and pepper on both sides of the smelt.**
- **Prepare the egg mix in a bowl.**
- **Heat vegetable oil in a wok to about 320° F (160° C).**
- **Toss the smelt in flour and gently shake off excess. Dip the smelt into the egg mix briefly and then into the panko. Make sure the panko covers the smelt entirely.**
- **Slip the smelt into the hot oil and cook until the coating turns a golden brown.**
- **Serve with a mound of thin-sliced cabbage or salad of your choice with a very light dressing.**

Smelt Tataki Salad

2 SERVINGS

4 filets smelt
1 teaspoon grated ginger
2 tablespoons chopped
green onions
2 shiso leaves thinly sliced
The squeezed juice of ¼ of
a lemon

Here's a recipe that incorporates raw smelt in a zesty mix of ingredients. Perfect for a summer meal on the porch. The word "*tataki*" means to hit or pound and often refers to mincing into very small pieces, but in this case, the smelt will be in more or less uniform 1" slices.

- **Remove the skin of a lightly salted and opened smelt.**
- **Slice the smelt into 1" length pieces.**
- **Mix the smelt with ginger, green onions and shiso.**
- **Add the lemon juice, toss lightly and serve.**

Smelt Sugatayaki

1 SERVING

2 smelt (the bigger the better —
about 1.75 oz per fish or more)
Salt, lemon
1 tablespoon grated daikon radish
4 bamboo skewers

This recipe calls for broiling or grilling the smelt. The word "*sugatayaki*" is a combination of the words "shape" (*sugata*) and "grill" (*yaki*), and it implies that the thing that is being grilled retains its original shape. Thus the whole smelt (or shrimp or squid or what have you) is grilled on a skewer.

You could try this recipe on your barbecue too. For a fancier presentation, apply the skewer, with the smelt forming a gentle curve. Cover the head and tail with aluminum foil when cooking to protect the ends from burning.

- Lightly salt both sides of the fish.
- Pierce two skewers about half an inch apart, through the mouth down the length of the fish.
- Moisten the tail and cover it with salt to protect it from burning.
- Turn the broiler on high heat and cook both sides on the second rack for a few minutes until lightly browned (keep an eye on the fish as it browns quickly.)
- Place the fish on a plate and turn the skewers gently to remove.
- Serve with a small mound of grated daikon and soy sauce on the side, garnished with a slice of lemon.

INGREDIENTS

2 liters water

60 grams shaved dried
bonito

40 grams konbu

10 **SHIRO'S TIPS**
HOW TO
EXTRACT DASHI

Delicious miso soup, clear broth and Japanese
nimono stews with meat, seafood and vegetables
all rely on a good *dashi*, or soup base. While
most Japanese households use pre-made dashi,
there's nothing better than a good dashi made
from scratch. Dashi is responsible for the *umami*
(savoriness) in Japanese cuisine.

The most commonly used dashi is an extract of
katsuobushi (dried bonito flakes) and *konbu* (brown
algae or seaweed). Instead of dried bonito, you
can use dried tuna, mackerel, sardines, small
sardines, chicken stock or dried mushrooms.
They all can make an excellent dashi.

- In a large pot, combine water with the konbu
  and cook on high heat.
- Just before the water begins to boil, remove
  the konbu.
- When the water comes to a boil, add a little bit
  of water to settle it down and add all the dried
  bonito to the pot at once and turn off the heat.
- When the dried bonito begins to settle to the
  bottom of the pot, put a cloth over a sieve and
  strain the broth into a bowl.

Filleting

Many of my recipes call for filleting. I have provided instructions on how to fillet the fish mentioned in each of the recipes for the adventurous cooks, but I also understand that unless you fish for a living, most readers might feel a little squeamish about handling fish guts. Luckily, most large supermarkets with a dedicated fish department will clean and fillet the fish for you. If not, most white fish mentioned in the recipes are sold as filets anyway, with the exception of smelt. Asian supermarkets in the International District carry fresh ocean smelt, but it is not as widespread as salmon or halibut.

Marinated Tuna Donburi

This dish can be made with any kind of tuna. It's typically made with bluefin tuna, but in the Pacific Northwest, albacore tuna makes a tasty substitute. A lot of people think of albacore as the tuna-fish tuna — the cans of tuna you use for tuna sandwiches. But the albacore is a delicious and under-rated sushi fish. The bluefin has good marketing behind it, so it has risen to exorbitant prices as the stock of bluefin tunas dwindles dangerously. The albacore is plentiful, affordable and delicious, so it's the natural choice for this dish in the Northwest.

4 SERVINGS

1 lb tuna sashimi unsliced
4 bowls cooked sushi rice
¼ cup shredded nori
wasabi

SAUCE

½ cup soy sauce
½ cup sake
Optional: 2 shiso leaves shredded, pickled ginger

- **Begin preparing the sushi rice, then make the sauce in a small bowl and set aside.**
- **Diagonally cut the tuna into sushi-size slices measuring ⅛" × 2 ½". When slicing the tuna, angle the blade and draw the knife towards you.**
- **Marinate the tuna in the sauce for 15-20 minutes — the fattier the tuna, the closer to 20 minutes.**
- **When you are ready to eat, serve warm sushi rice in each of the bowls, sprinkle the nori and evenly portion out the tuna slices over it. Squeeze a small amount of wasabi onto the side of the bowl.**
- **Optional: Sprinkle shiso leaves and serve with pickled ginger on the side.**

Poke Belltown

4 SERVINGS

1 lb tuna sashimi

2 tablespoons chopped green onions

⅓ cup ponzu

½ teaspoon chili oil

1 teaspoon sriracha

¼ teaspoon sansho powder

½ tablespoon wasabi mayonnaise mix (1:4 ratio)

1 tablespoon tobiko (flying fish roe)

Poke is a Hawaiian dish made with ahi yellowfin tuna, chili oil, Maui onions, green onions and other ingredients, including flying fish roe, or *tobiko*. "*Poke*" means "to cut" in Hawaiian. I made a twist on the dish by adding some Thai spices, ponzu sauce, a wasabi-mayo mix and some Japanese pepper, and named it after the neighborhood where Shiro's is. It's easy to make, healthy and delicious. A house favorite.

- **Slice a well-refrigerated tuna into ½" thick cubes.**
- **Place the cubed tuna in a bowl along with all the other ingredients and mix gently.**
- **Eat!**

Salmon Skin Salad

4 SERVINGS

½ lb salmon skin

½ cup liquid smoke

2 stalks green onion, chopped

2 tablespoons tobiko (flying fish roe)

2 oz dried wakame (seaweed)

⅓ English cucumber sliced

¾ cup ponzu

2 teaspoons roasted sesame

½ bunch sprouts

Lemon wedge

Optional: Hot sauce

For this dish, remember to set aside 2 hours to marinate.

Salmon skin is hard to come by. This is not generally sold in markets, but you can visit your favorite fish shop in the afternoon and ask for any leftover salmon skin.

- Remove the scales from the salmon skin using a wire brush. Don't worry about removing every little scale because baking will take care of the rest.
- Soak the salmon skin in a dish or pan for 2 hours in liquid smoke.
- Turn the broiler on high and cook the salmon skin until lightly browned on both sides. This process makes the skin very crispy. (At Shiro's, we refrigerate the cooked skin overnight; it makes it easy to shred into very thin slices.)
- Chop up the green onions and let sit in running water for 5 minutes. During this time, also soak wakame in a bowl of water for 5 minutes or until softened. Drain both to remove excess water.
- Slice the cucumber lengthwise in half, remove the seeds, and cut into thin slices. Toss the cucumbers in a bowl with salt, then rinse in clean water and drain.
- Cut the cooked salmon skin into 1½" × ⅛" slices. (At the restaurant, we reheat the salmon skin slices in the oven to bring back the crunchiness).
- Pour ponzu sauce into a bowl and add the salmon skin, chopped green onions, the flying fish roe, wakame and cucumbers. Add the optional hot sauce, too, if you like, and toss until well mixed.
- Transfer to a serving plate and sprinkle roasted sesame and sprouts on top.

Garnish with a wedge of lemon and serve.

Chawan Mushi Shiro Style

Chawan mushi is a savory egg custard dish that is usually served in a special china cup with a lid. If you have a regular teacup with a lid, that will work too. I've also seen some recipes that use a cloth to cover the top, which may be worth a try, but to be honest, I've never made the dish in anything but chawan mushi cups. Just remember that whatever you use has to be able to be steamed, so don't use lacquerware.

This particular recipe calls for shrimp, but you can use chicken or white fish instead. You can also use a chicken broth instead of the *dashi* base I use. A versatile meal, this hearty appetizer is perfect on a cold winter's night. Or on any day in Seattle that's grey and overcast.

4 SERVINGS

4 chawan mushi cups with lids
1 steamer
—
4 eggs
2 ½ cups dashi base
⅓ teaspoon mirin
⅓ teaspoon salt
⅓ teaspoon low-sodium soy sauce
4 shrimp peeled and de-veined
1 stalk mitsuba cut into 4 small portions or 4 boiled spinach leaves
2 tablespoons shredded matsutake or shiitake mushrooms
Optional: 4 ginkgo biloba seeds

- **Combine dashi base with mirin, salt and low-sodium soy sauce.**
- **Beat the eggs and add to the sauce made above, then filter the mixture through a sieve.**
- **Evenly portion into the four individual cups shrimp, mitsuba/spinach and matsutake/shiitake mushrooms. Gently pour the combination of sauce and eggs into the cups, removing froth that collects at the top (this is important), then put a lid on the cups.**
- **Carefully place the cups into a preheated steamer and cook on high heat for about 9 minutes. Then gently poke a thin bamboo stick down the center of the chawan mushi. If the liquid that rushes to the top is clear, it is done.**

*If possible, use matsutake mushrooms; they have an earthier scent and taste that are a big part of this dish.

Scallops and Matsutake Broiled in Aluminum Foil

1 SERVING

2 (2 oz) slices rockfish or any
other white fish

2 scallops

1 medium-size matsutake sliced

2 stalks asparagus boiled

1 teaspoon butter

1 tablespoon flour

Vegetable oil

Salt

Pepper

½ teaspoon sake

1 slice lemon

This recipe can be prepared with any local white fish. The matsutake infuses this dish with an earthiness that goes so well with the scallops and the asparagus. I used to make this dish after my son and I went matsutake-picking in the Cascades.

- Lightly salt and flour the scallops and set aside. Melt butter in a medium fry pan on high heat and sear the scallops until browned on both sides.
- Set the broiler to 500° F (260° C).
- Grease an 8" × 10" sheet of aluminum foil with vegetable oil.
- Add in the center of the aluminum foil 2-3 slices of the matsutake, then lightly salt the white fish and layer over the matsutake. Cover the fish with the remaining matsutake. Dribble sake over the mixture and add the asparagus and scallops.
- Gently wrap the fish and vegetables with the aluminum foil.
- Broil the wrap for 8-9 minutes.
- Eat while hot, using ponzu as a sauce.

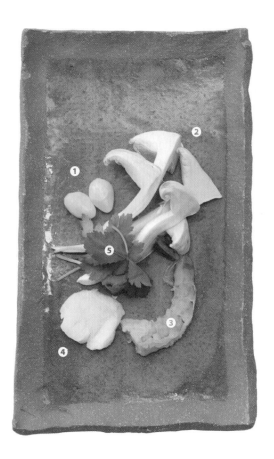

1 Ginkgo biloba seeds
2 Matsutake
3 Shrimp
4 White fish
5 Mitsuba leaves
6 Lime

Matsutake Dobin Mushi

4 SERVINGS

6 oz filet of white fish (red
snapper, rockfish or halibut)

1 lb matsutake mushrooms

4 shrimp unpeeled, but with the
head removed

12 ginkgo biloba seeds (available
at Asian supermarkets in canned
form)

⅓ bunch spinach leaves or
mitsuba leaves

BROTH

3 cups dashi base

½ teaspoon salt

½ teaspoon light soy sauce

1 teaspoon sake

1 lime quartered

Dobin mushi is a Japanese broth served in a teapot. I love
making this when the matsutake are in season because it
really brings out the essence of those earthy mushrooms.
In Japanese, we say *"kaori o taberu,"* which means "eat the
flavor" or "imbibe the aroma." That's a key to enjoying
this dish. The little pots used for this recipe are sold at
most Japanese grocery stores.

- **Heat water in a saucepan until it boils. Prepare a bowl of
  cold water.**
- **Slice the filet of white fish into 1" × ½" slices, dip briefly in
  boiling water then quickly transfer into a bowl of cold water.**
- **Remove the hard base of the matsutake, and clean with a
  wet cloth in gentle strokes.**
- **Slice the matsutake into 2-2½" × ½" slices and set aside.**
- **Blanch the shrimp briefly in hot water and place in cold
  water. When the shrimp cools off, remove the shell (but
  keep the tail on) and de-vein.**
- **Boil the spinach briefly and cool off in cold running water,
  then gently squeeze excess water before cutting them into
  2" slices.**
- **Prepare the broth by combining dashi base in a medium-size
  saucepan with salt, light soy sauce and sake. Check for taste,
  adding more salt or soy sauce as necessary, then pour the
  broth into a large dobin mushi pot and set aside.**
- **Prepare a steamer with boiling water.**
- **While waiting for the steamer, add white fish, matsutake,
  shrimp and flesh of ginkgo biloba seeds in the teapot. When
  the steamer is ready, place the teapot in the steamer and
  cook for 9-10 minutes with the lid on.**
- **Slice the lime into 4 parts and place them on top of the
  teapot with the lid turned upside down.**
- **Serve in a teacup and squeeze the lime over the broth for
  fragrance.**

1 Hakusai cabbage
2 White fish
3 Shiitake mushroom
4 Enoki mushroom
5 Green onion
6 Tofu

Nabe Mono

1 whole white fish
Anything local, like snapper,
halibut or rockfish. If you are
uneasy about cleaning fish, ask the
fish store where you purchase the
fish to remove the scales and clean
the fish, but do not throw away the
head. Ask them to chop the head
up into a few chunks to bring home.

10 or so leaves hakusai cabbage
1 bunch green onions
6-8 fresh shiitake mushrooms
1 pack enoki mushrooms
4 matsutake roughly sliced (if
available)
1 pack harusame (cellophane
noodles)
1 pack tofu
10 cm square konbu
seaweed sheet

PONZU DIP MIXTURE

per serving:
¼ cup ponzu
1 tablespoon grated daikon
1 teaspoon minced green onions
Cayenne or shichimi pepper
(optional)

This dish is traditionally prepared at the dining table on top of a heating source. It's a great meal on a cold night or during those grey Seattle winter days. It's also a lot of fun because everyone pitches in and cooks together. Children especially like this way of eating.

I loaded up this recipe with lots of mushrooms, but there are unlimited variations you can make with this dish. Put in your favorite ingredients and give it a try.

- **Cut the fish lengthwise in half, then chop the flesh into large chunks.**
- **Dip the fish in lightly salted hot water for 30 seconds and replace in cold water.**
- **Slice hakusai cabbage and green onions into 2-3" lengths.**
- **Remove the base of the matsutake and let cellophane noodles sit in water until softened.**
- **Arrange all the ingredients — the fish, vegetables, tofu, cellophane noodles and mushrooms — on a large serving plate.**
- **Place the konbu in a Japanese *nabe* — large, shallow pot — and fill the pot about 70% full with water and cook on medium heat until boiling. Then add the fish head, flesh and bones. Take out the konbu before the water comes to a full boil. Then remove the froth that collects at the top using a ladle and continue cooking on medium heat for 12-13 minutes.**
- **Start by adding about ⅓ of the flesh part of the fish, then add the vegetables, tofu, cellophane noodles and mushrooms. Continue cooking until the stew comes to a boil. Add remaining fish and vegetables slowly as needed.**
- **Add spices to the ponzu sauce, and use as a dip. Enjoy.**

Kinki (Idiot Fish) Nitsuke

1 kinki about ½ lb in size

½ cup sake

½ cup water

⅓ cup soy sauce

2 tablespoons mirin

2 tablespoons sugar

Remember the Patagonian toothfish? It swam around the South American waters in blissful obscurity until a marketing whiz decided to rename it the Chilean seabass. All of a sudden, it was a gourmet meal, and the former toothfish had to swim for their lives.

Well, the idiot fish has so far evaded the marketing gurus. It's a tasty white fish that is popular in Japan and indigenous to the Pacific Northwest. This recipe calls for it to be cooked *nitsuke* style, which means it is simmered in a mixture of mirin, sake, water, soy sauce and sugar. You can use this recipe on all sorts of white fish — try red snapper, halibut or rockfish, for example — but it's especially good with the cleverly named idiot fish. Let's hope the marketing gurus leave this name alone.

- Remove the scales, the innards, the head and wash in clean water. Remove excess water with a clean cloth.
- Place the head to your left, then use a knife to make two incisions on the side so it cooks faster and the flavor seeps in. (Most supermarkets will clean the fish for you if you prefer not to do this procedure yourself.)
- In a shallow pan with a lid, combine the sake, water, soy sauce, mirin and sugar, and cook until boiling.
- Place the fish in the pan and cook on medium high heat for 5-6 minutes with the lid on.
- Remove the lid, raise the heat a little and use a ladle to scoop the broth over the fish for 3-4 minutes. This allows the flavor to sink in and create a sheen on the fish.
- Remove the fish onto a plate, pour the broth over the fish and serve.

WINTER SEAFOOD

❶ Bahun uni

❷ Murasaki uni

❸ Petrale sole

❹ Kinki (idiot fish)

❺ Squid

❻ Rex sole

11 SHIRO'S TIPS
RIVER FISH VERSUS
OCEAN FISH

In Seattle, there are plenty of sushi bars that serve raw salmon. I highly recommend that you don't indulge unless you know that it has been flash-frozen first. I'm afraid that in some establishments, that process is skipped because the chefs don't know their fish.

Not any fish can be eaten raw and fresh. Sometimes, for safety's sake, it's necessary to lightly grill or flash-freeze a fish to kill the bacteria and parasites inside. It's the same reason we started cooking meat long ago.

Salmon (and many other river fish) are highly susceptible to parasites. The flash-freezing process kills them off. Plus, it still tastes great. So make sure you or your sushi chef don't skip this process.

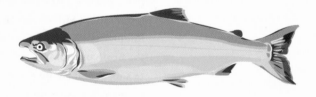

Salmon Misoyaki

4 SERVINGS

4 salmon filets

MISO SAUCE

¾ lb white miso
½ cup sugar
⅓ cup mirin
⅓ cup sake
2 large sheets of gauze or very
thin linen (enough to cover four
salmon filets)

This recipe requires marination for 12 to 24 hours. The rest is simple.

This recipe is wonderful for fattier fish such as swordfish and Patagonian tooth … I mean Chilean seabass.

- **Lightly salt both sides of the salmon filets.**
- **Mix the miso, sugar, mirin and sake in a medium size bowl.**
- **Pour ½ of the miso sauce into a baking dish and place a sheet of gauze over the sauce. Lay the salmon filets side by side. Put another sheet of gauze over the salmon and pour the rest of the miso sauce on top. Refrigerate for 12 to 24 hours.**
- **Remove the miso sauce and gauze and check the salmon to make sure there is no miso residue on them. If there is, use a clean cloth to wipe off or lightly rinse under running water to remove traces of the miso sauce.**
- **Place the salmon filets in a pan and cook both sides slowly on medium heat. The marinade makes the salmon easier to burn, so keep an eye on it.**

Salmon Teriyaki

4 SERVINGS

4 filets fresh salmon (weighing about 4-4.5 oz each)

TERIYAKI SAUCE:
1 tablespoon sugar
½ tablespoon mirin
2½ tablespoons sake
2½ tablespoons light soy sauce
½ tablespoon vegetable oil

I never saw so much teriyaki until I came to Seattle! Of course we have teriyaki in Japan — it's a Japanese cooking style, after all — but not to the extent that Seattle has embraced it. So here's a dish that's about as Seattle as you can get: salmon teriyaki.

- Combine sugar, mirin, sake and light soy sauce in a bowl and mix.
- In a large fry pan, heat oil and cook the salmon skin-side down in medium heat. Be careful not to burn the skin. Turn over when it turns a golden brown color and repeat on the other side.
- Set aside the salmon and remove oil from the frying pan.
- Wipe clean the frying pan and cook the teriyaki sauce until gently boiling, then add the salmon.
- Turn the heat down to low for a minute or two and ladle the teriyaki sauce over the fish while gently rocking the pan so as not to burn the salmon or the sauce.
- Be careful not to overcook the salmon.

Rex Sole Shioyaki

1 SERVING

1 rex sole, cleaned and with head
and tail removed
1 tablespoon grated daikon
1 slice lemon
Salt

Rex sole and grated daikon radish is a match made in heaven.

- **Remove the scales of the fish and wash in running water.**
- **Remove excess moisture with a cloth or paper towel.**
- **Sprinkle a pinch of salt on both sides.**
- **Lightly grease aluminum foil and spread over cooking sheet.**
- **Set the broiler to high and cook the sole with the lighter side of the flesh facing up to about ¾ done on the middle rack.**
- **Turn over and cook until lightly brown.**
- **Transfer the sole to a dish and serve with grated daikon and lemon on the side.**

Rex Sole Karaage Shiro Style

1 SERVING

1 rex sole (cleaned) about ½ lb
3 tablespoons ponzu
3 cups vegetable oil or just
enough to crisply fry the fish
½ cup potato starch
Salt

MOMIJI OROSHI

1 tablespoon grated daikon
A sprinkle of red pepper powder
or Japanese ichimi spice

When deep-frying fish or seafood, for instance, the fish will float up to the surface after awhile. That's a sign that the fish has been sufficiently cooked. Just before it bobs up to the surface, big bubbles give way to smaller bubbles. When the bubbles disappear, the fish will float up.

If you are particular about the texture of fried fish and you want to achieve that crispy tenderness, removing the fish from the oil at the right time is paramount. Leave the fish in too long to assure doneness and you could end up with something dry and lacking in fragrance, and worst of all, with no taste.

Also, you'll see something called *momiji oroshi* in this recipe. The word "momiji" refers to the deep red or golden hues of the autumn leaves. "Oroshi" refers to the grating process. Simple homemade momiji oroshi can be prepared with one hot red pepper, softened in water, and a 3-4" section of peeled daikon radish. Carefully remove the seeds from the red pepper without breaking it up. Using a chopstick, drill a hole about the size of the red pepper into the curved side of the daikon, and grate. The pigment from the red pepper turns the daikon into a golden color with little bits of red that resemble the colors of the autumn leaves.

Also, when we remove the bones from a fish, we make a crispy bone *sembei*, which is a tasty treat. We soak the fish bones in salt water for two hours to replicate the saltiness of seawater. Then we hang the fish bones to dry in the kitchen for about 3 days to remove moisture. This ensures extra crispiness.

Remove the scales from the rex sole and prepare the fish so that it is sliced into three sections in a method called *sanmai oroshi* in Japanese:

1 First, remove the head and clean the fish.
2 Position the fish with the belly away from you. If you are right-handed, place the head side to your right. Make an incision along the back, where the dorsal fin is, and slide the knife flat along the top of the spine. Relax your hand and try not to apply too much pressure or the knife can slice through the bones. Do the same with the belly side until the flesh has separated from the spine.
3 Flip the fish over and repeat the process until you have two filets and the fish bones.

- Sprinkle salt over the cleaned and filleted fish.
- Peel the daikon and grate. Drain excess moisture and mix in red pepper or Japanese ichimi powder.
- Lightly sprinkle potato starch over the fish and set aside.
- Heat vegetable oil in a wok until hot (about 370° F, or 190° C). Dip the fish into the oil and let cook for 5-6 minutes. Add the fish bone to the oil and wait until it floats to the surface, then cook an additional 5 minutes.
- Remove the fish and the fish bone onto a plate lined with paper towels to absorb excess oil. Lightly salt the fish bone.
- Serve with a small mound of momiji oroshi daikon on the side.
- Prepare a small dish of ponzu to spoon over the momiji oroshi as desired.

Calamari Somen Shiro Style

1 SERVING

3-4 fresh local squid

1 teaspoon size fresh sea urchin

¼ teaspoon wasabi

½ tablespoon shredded nori

Soy sauce

1 quail egg

One day I was out on a boat with some American friends, lazing away on the Sound. We were fishing, and someone reeled in a little squid. I took out my knife and hacked off a bit to have a taste. It was delicious. But my friends were looking at me with horror. I must have seemed like some sort of barbarian! So this recipe goes out to my American fishing buddies.

- Slice only the top layer of the squid lengthwise to spread it open. Remove the cartilage and the legs and dispose.
- Flatten the squid on a cutting board so the inside faces up. Make a 1" incision straight across the bottom quarter on the inside part of the squid.
- Flip the squid over and lift the bottom portion where the incision was made and pull the outer skin off with one hand while pinning the calamari down with the other hand. Pull the skin off in an upward motion.
- Turn the squid over once more to expose the inside. Peel off or use a dry towel to rub off the translucent membrane.
- With the squid flat on the cutting board, cut it into thin, ⅛" slices lengthwise (think of somen or angel hair pasta).
- Transfer the thin-sliced squid into a serving bowl.
- Sprinkle shredded nori over it and top it with a fresh uni.
- Make a small depression in the center of the uni, and place a raw quail egg on top.
- Serve with wasabi and soy sauce on the side.

To eat, gently mix the squid with a little bit of wasabi and soy sauce.

Braised Local Calamari

4 SERVINGS

16 fresh local calamari (frozen
calamari work fine too)

BROTH

5 cups water

¾ cup soy sauce

¾ cup mirin

¼ cup sake

12 pcs of ginger, sliced

- Combine ingredients for the broth in a shallow cooking pan.
- Clean the squid by firmly but carefully pulling out the legs and using pincers to remove the cartilage inside the body.
- In a separate medium-size pan, bring water to a boil and cook the calamari with its legs stuffed inside its body for 5-10 seconds, then transfer to ice cold water.
- Add the calamari to the broth and heat to a boil. Turn the heat down before the mixture begins to boil. After 6-8 minutes, the calamari will float to the surface.
- Turn off the heat.
- Serve with steamed asparagus and tofu.
  (The squid is good for 2 to 3 days)

Saba (Mackerel)

There are three types of mackerel served at restaurants around Seattle: the Norwegian mackerel, Spanish mackerel from Japan, Hawaii or California, and the King mackerel also from Japan or the Atlantic Ocean. I would like to share the recipes for three very popular *saba* dishes. I recommend the frozen Norwegian mackerel because it is fattier and oilier, since it travels in colder waters. This is an exception to my usual rule of going local, but this mackerel is just too tasty to pass up.

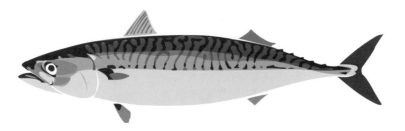

Shime Saba

2 SERVINGS

1 Norwegian mackerel

1 cup salt

3 cups rice vinegar

This simple yet delicious meal needs to be prepared 3½ hours in advance. After the usual cleaning procedure and filleting, the fish has to be marinated in salt for three hours. Then it needs to sit in vinegar for at least another 30 minutes. If you have the time, let the mackerel sit overnight. The vinegar seeps into the flesh for a truly delicious finish.

- **Clean the fish, remove the head and fillet into three parts: two filets and the bone.**
- **Sprinkle ½ cup of salt on each filet and let sit for three hours.**
- **After the marination, rinse off salt gently under running water. The mackerel has soft flesh, so handle with care.**
- **Gently pat dry, then place in a pan and pour in rice vinegar until the mackerel is just about completely covered. Let sit for at least 30 minutes.**
- **Place mackerel into a strainer to let the vinegar drain. Then place the fish on a cutting board and remove the bones at the center of the flesh with tweezers.**
- **A thin, translucent film covers the skin of the mackerel. Remove this film by tugging on a corner near the side of the head and pulling it toward the tail.**
- **It's now ready as sashimi (slice into thin pieces), sushi or for the grill.**

Saba Shioyaki

4 SERVINGS

1 Norwegian mackerel

1 lemon, cut into 4 wedges

1 teaspoon salt

½ cup grated daikon

4 tsp soy sauce

"Shioyaki" means grilled *(yaki)* with salt *(shio)*.

- **Remove the head and clean the fish. Rinse well under running water.**
- **Position the fish with the belly away from you. Place the head side to your right. Start with an incision along the back, where the dorsal fin is, and slide the knife flat along the top of the spine toward the tail, drawing the blade toward you. Remove the filet and set aside. Turn the fish over and repeat the same process until you have two filets and the bone. Remove the bones attached to the belly.**
- **Cut the filet into four pieces.**
- **Sprinkle each piece with ¼ teaspoon of the salt.**
- **Cover a baking pan with aluminum foil and grease the foil.**
- **Set the broiler to 450° F (232° C) and bake with the skin side up until the fish is a little more than half done, about 7-8 minutes. Then turn over and cook 4-5 minutes until done.**
- **Serve each filet with a mound of grated daikon. Add a splash of soy sauce on top and a lemon wedge on the side.**

Mackerel Cooked in Misoni

4 SERVINGS

1 Norwegian mackerel cleaned
and cut into 4 pieces

2 small knobs of fresh ginger
root, peeled and thinly sliced

6 stalks green onions, chopped
into 1 ½" pieces

¼ cup sake

¼ cup water

2 to 3 oz red miso paste

3 tablespoons dashi

2 tablespoons sugar

1 teaspoon soy sauce

Misoni is a cooking style that simmers the fish in a broth and brings a warm depth to the soft flesh of the mackerel. This recipe can also be replicated with other white fish like rockfish and red snapper.

- **In a large pot, combine sake, water, thinly sliced ginger and mackerel cut into four pieces, and cook on high heat for 10 minutes.**
- **Combine in a bowl the miso with the dashi. Add sugar and soy sauce into the bowl, then pour the content into the pot and cook for about 4 minutes.**
- **Add the green onions and cook for 1 or 2 minutes.**
- **Eat.**

Index

Acknowledgments

This project would never have been realized without the incredible vision and wordsmithing genius of Bruce Rutledge and Yuko Enomoto and their entire staff at Chin Music Press — in particular, Josh Powell, whose love of the Japanese culture radiates through his art direction, as well as the photographic mastery of Ann Norton, which takes my creations and lifts them to a whole other level.

Chin Music's dedication to maintaining the art of the hard copy book is the exact same philosophy I have with my cooking. There could not have been a better collaboration to bring this project to fruition. You could say we were absolutely all "on the same page."

I also would like to thank the Shiro's Sushi Kitchen Group for all of their help and encouragement throughout this year-long process.

I am grateful to my family back in Kyoto whose love and support, no matter how far apart we are, has been a sense of comfort to me throughout my life. Special thanks to my sisters Eiko and Mitsuko, who helped dig up old photographs for this book, some of which I didn't even know existed. And finally, of course, to my wife Ricky and son Edwin whose enthusiasm and unconditional love makes every day a joy to live.

Kumamoto castle

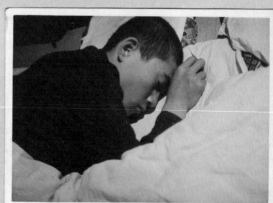

Nagasaki